COMMUNITY AND MINISTRY

COMMUNITY AND MINISTRY

An introduction to community development in a Christian context

SPCK Library of Ministry

PAUL BALLARD
and
LESLEY HUSSELBEE

First published in Great Britain in 2007

Society for Promoting Christian Knowledge
36 Causton Street
London SW1P 4ST

British Library Cataloguing-in-Publication Data
A catalogue record for this book is available from the British Library

ISBN 978–0–281–05800–6

1 3 5 7 9 10 8 6 4 2

Typeset by Graphicraft Ltd, Hong Kong
Printed in Great Britain by Ashford Colour Press

Produced on paper from sustainable forests

Contents

Part II
WORKING WITH ORGANIZATIONS AND PEOPLE

Figures

Acknowledgements

Two kinds of acknowledgements need to be made. First, every reasonable effort has been taken to ensure that copyright has not been infringed. All the figures and diagrams have been produced especially for this publication based on the information from the sources indicated at each point. We are specifically grateful for permission to use material from *Assets for Life* (London, URC, Church Related Community Work Desk, 2004) and *Straat voor Straat. Delphi Opbouwerk. Door straataanpak meer sociale binding* (Rotterdam, Stichting Opbouwerk, 2004). In the event of any inadvertent breach of copyright being communicated to the publishers, the situation will be rectified and due acknowledgement made.

The second is to express gratitude to those who in various ways have made the writing of this book possible. No book emerges in a vacuum. A debt is owed to many who down the years have been our mentors and colleagues. However, as members of the Consultation on the Church Related Community Work Course Development in Northern College and Luther King Open College, Manchester, it has been especially valuable to have the interest and encouragement of the group and other members of staff. Similarly there has been the generous help given during Lesley's visits to many significant projects during sabbatical leave. As always, too, there are those in the background without whose long-suffering support nothing would get done. So thanks are sincerely due to Gerrie (wife) and Maurice (husband), who have borne the heat and burden of coping with authorial strain. Similarly a real debt is due to Ruth McCurry and the team at SPCK who have been wise and patient in bringing the whole enterprise to fruition.

Paul Ballard
Lesley Husselbee
Lent 2007

Introduction

Community work and the churches

Community work in the churches

In many an English parish church it is possible to see lists of charitable bequests for the relief of the poor. These are reminders that the Church has been, for many generations, the hub of community life. The parson was often the magistrate and school teacher and administered the parish welfare system, part of the fabric of law and order and integral to the well-being of the parish. This Reformation pattern can be traced back into medieval Christendom, when the Church, not least through the network of monastic and other orders, ministered to the poor and the sick – a concern that can be found in the earliest days of the Church, showing forth Christ's compassion on all. Catholicism, for its part, also developed ways of working in the wider society, not least through the new charitable, educational and nursing orders that emerged out of the Counter-Reformation and in the local parish through its clubs and welfare societies, such as the Society of St Vincent de Paul. Again, British Nonconformity provided, through the chapel, means of education and mutual welfare that are one of the roots of modern democratic society.

All that, however, has been radically changed under the impact of two major influences that have shaped modern society. First, the Industrial Revolution and the rise of the great conurbations created a sense of the collapse of manageable community and the fragmentation of society. It is no accident that this concern was a major factor in the emergence of sociology, from Marx to Durkheim and Weber. Each, in his own way, was a prophet against the woes of the modern world and its dehumanization. Second, and closely linked, was the process of secularization, at least in the particular sense of the decoupling of social functions from under the auspices of the Church. Through the nineteenth century and beyond, education, welfare and health all became the responsibility of the state, climaxing in the golden age of the Welfare State (1945–80). In such ways the Church has been shifted from the centre to the margins, from the public sphere to the private, from the communal to the individual. The process has never been complete and, as we shall presently see, can be and is being questioned. The general effect, however, has been for the churches to find themselves part of the voluntary sector, at best working alongside the statutory authorities. This does not mean that we should dismiss the often impressive and sometimes decisive contributions, over this whole period of turbulent change, made for the good of society by Christian leaders, philanthropists and pioneers, from enacting laws to providing housing, from working with the poor and destitute to struggling for human rights, from mass education to health and safety.

The second half of the twentieth century, however, saw another factor that needs to be noted here. As part of the post-war reconstruction which shaped the Welfare State, there was a deep commitment to planning. Urban renewal after the destruction of war, coupled with a determination to do away with the industrial slums, meant creating new communities, including new towns and overspill housing estates, and reconstructing the inner city. Whatever the shortcomings in practice, this has been a major factor in shaping our contemporary society. It also meant that community facilities, such as youth and sports centres and even churches, were part of the new provision. Out of and alongside this came community work. It was apparent that, because of such far-reaching changes, reinforced in the seventies by the decline in traditional industries, received community patterns were breaking down. Attention had to be given to building community afresh. Appointments were made by local authorities, especially in youth and community work, but also of community development officers whose remit was to facilitate the development of community structures in those places to which people had suddenly been moved or whose communities had been radically reshaped. A new, though small, professional group had thus come into being.

Not surprisingly, the churches also took up this concern. A considerable number of new churches were planted in the new estates and towns, many of which became involved in the formation of community groups, working with the authorities in different ways. In the older areas there was often a chance to renew premises, making them suitable as community centres and introducing new programmes. Moreover there were opportunities to appoint community workers, not infrequently at the local authority's expense. All this was seen as a natural development of the long-standing provision by the churches of community facilities and involvement, exemplified in the Salvation Army and the orders of religious and deaconesses found in several denominations. But it also now meant appropriating the emerging professional community work model. So there was a growing number of church-related community workers who saw themselves as exercising a specialist ministry. This was acknowledged by the setting up of a Community Work Resource Unit in the British Council of Churches (BCC) supported by the Home Office to promote community work among the churches. It was disbanded at the demise of the BCC in 1990, but its work has been continued through the Churches' Community Work Alliance (CCWA). The United Reformed Church (URC) in fact officially recognized community work as a form of authorized ministry and it has a small but active group of Church Related Community Workers (CRCW) stationed across the country.

Since 1980, however, there have been three further developments on the national scene. First, the election of the Thatcher government in 1979 signalled the advent of the full-blown market economy and the erosion, if not the dismantling, of the Welfare State. One of the results has been the rapid widening of the gap between the rich and poor in society and the rise in the indices of poverty such as homelessness. This has been exacerbated by the deindustrialization of Britain. In reaction to this, alongside other voices, came the protest of *Faith in the City* (1985) from the Church of England, focusing on the decaying state of much of the inner city and many of the peripheral working-class housing estates. Here, then, was a rallying cry for renewed interest in the breakdown of community. This was the trigger for the establishment, in the Church of England, of the Church Urban Fund and the Commission on Urban Life and Faith, now working ecumenically, which have continued to stimulate reflection and action, most recently in the report *Faithful Cities* (2006).

The second development has been the approach of New Labour since 1997. The so-called 'third way' seeks to combine the economic priority of market forces with targeted and increased resources to address the problems of social exclusion, such as poverty and disability, with a view to maximizing the economic use of human and material potential. Integral to this policy has been a 'consumerist' shift in welfare provision. This leads to a call for a greater collaboration between the statutory, commercial and voluntary sectors, including the churches and other faith groups. Indeed, many churches and other Christian enterprises have taken up this challenge, from small local projects to national organizations. It looks as though, after long years of marginalization, Cinderella is being invited back to the ball, but on very different terms from those that pertained before.

Yet there is a certain irony here. The churches have become aware of their acute institutional decline and therefore lack of resources to put into fresh initiatives. But there are signs that this coincidence can work for a renewal. As the churches are having to become ever more aware of their need to relate to and address a very different society, so they are experimenting, formally and informally, nationally and locally, within and beyond the accepted structures, with new forms of ministry and fresh ways of operating. The openings afforded by collaborative partnerships in community, social, welfare and educational provision come just at the right time. One of these, central to our present concerns in this book, is the thrust to redefine local ministry in terms of 'community ministry', reconfiguring the relationship between congregation and the local community. This is the third contemporary impetus towards recognizing the importance of community work for Christian ministry.

This, then, is the background for this study in community work, the congregation and its ministry. What it shows is that, at this time, there is considerable and lively engagement with the life of the local community in many congregations; perhaps as much as, or even more than ever. This both draws on past tradition and is yet a new development within that tradition. Especially must account be taken of the developments that are at the heart of modern community work.

What is community work?

Community work, as it has emerged in recent times, is one of the 'helping' or 'caring' professions that came on the scene with the Welfare State. It drew, like them, on the explosion of interest in the human sciences in and after the Second World War. There was, therefore, considerable common ground with such professions as social work, teaching and counselling. But it also developed its own cognitive and theoretical base and evolved its own skills and practices. The emphasis is on understanding the social dynamics of human existence; how people live and work and play together and create social relationships and a sense of identity. The individual is important, but here finds meaning from the group, to which he or she contributes. Because community work relates to social realities there is also a tendency to stress the social connections between the immediate situation and the wider society. This has meant that at times community work has veered towards the political, but is only thus reflecting the complex nexus of human existence.

Modern community work has, at least in part, its roots in late colonial administration, in programmes devised to enhance the economic position of traditional communities. Instead of imposing schemes for development, introducing high western technology, people like T. R. Batten started with the community and through involvement and dialogue helped them to decide for themselves what were the most important immediate needs and then to seek ways of working with them to meet that need. It may be to dig a well or create an irrigation system or to obtain better educational or health facilities. In other words development was from the ground up, engaging people and asking them to take responsibility. Community work, certainly as we understand it in this book, therefore, is primarily seen as 'community development'. Put simply, community work seeks to facilitate, in a given situation, a level of awareness and co-operation, so that people as a group can act together in such ways as to improve their common life. Community is thus developed both through the enhanced facilities or organizations or activities that emerge, and through the shared experience of working together that enables such developments to happen.

These were the principles that ministers and church workers encountered and began to introduce into their pastoral practice and mission in the neighbourhood, especially where they were working on the new estates or in the new towns. They found, as have others after them, that it affords a distinctive perspective that is both compatible with the gospel and relevant to key aspects of ministry, not least in building up the congregation and in creating a greater sense of neighbourhood in a pluralistic and changing society.

The aim and shape of the book

So what is being offered here is an introduction to the insights, skills and practices that are found in community development in order to relate them specifically to Christian witness and service in and through the local congregation. At a time when there is an increasing emphasis on new expressions of Church and a desire for the Christian community to engage with and work in the wider community, it is hoped that this will provide a useful resource. There is no quick fix or panacea for the problems facing mission today; but it is always well to search for the best tools available for the job.

At the forefront of our concern are ways and means whereby the churches can sponsor and support community initiatives, from major projects with paid, professional staff working with recruited volunteers, to the more normal but no less important small ventures run entirely by church members and their allies, and the ways in which the neighbourhood church can be a location for community activity. The primary audience, therefore, are those, full-time or part-time, involved in community work, or preparing to enter into it, in and with the churches. But it is also for those who support the community-related activities of their church, whether in management roles, or as leaders, such as the minister, deacon or elder, or simply as church members committed to action in and for the community, and who, perhaps, need to be more aware of what community work entails.

At the same time the contention is that community development perspectives and practices can and should inform every aspect of the life of the congregation. The local church, whatever form it takes, is itself a community. It is commonplace to talk of the Christian family but, it can be suggested, it would be better to think in terms of community. This image is more dynamic, allowing for the wide variety of belonging that is present in any one congregation and for a sense of journey and adventure. Communities need to be built up, both corporately and in and for their members. Community work can provide insights into the dynamics of leadership and participation, into aims and objectives both for the group and its individuals, that can enrich the shared life of faith and witness. Thus the issues raised and the perspectives offered are relevant to every aspect of ministry, from administration to worship, from Bible study with youth groups to pastoral encounters. This is true for both the ordained ministry and for anyone in a position of leadership within the congregation. Community work principles are about the whole ministry of the whole Church.

Third, there are those who are responsible for the wider structures of the churches, regionally and nationally. This is a time of scarce resources that need to be used wisely. It is, therefore, important to be able to recognize and evaluate and respond to the demands and needs of community work in order to deploy assets to the best advantage and to make considered appointments.

Fourth, the demands of theological education and ministerial training have been borne in mind. Concern for understanding and working with the community lies alongside pastoral care, leadership in worship, education and administration, and in the processes of professional and personal formation. The aim, then, has been to provide a basic introductory text, as well as a foundation for specialist studies.

All this, however, if it is to have a Christian perspective, has equally to be put within a process of theological reflection. Thus all the theoretical and practical issues are related to situations of mission and service. From time to time, too, there are explicit opportunities for theological reflection, with special emphasis on the biblical material. Attention is also specifically given to aspects of both personal and corporate spirituality.

Finally, community work is about people and their shared stories. Every effort has been made to earth the discussion in the concrete reality of life and ministry. This, too, reflects the contemporary interest in narrative theology. Situations and incidents, however, unless the information is in the public realm, have been kept anonymous and even conflated and reworked; but they are all based on experience and concrete realities. The stories, however, are more than case studies. They are the vehicle for reflection and carry the progression of the discussion. For this reason narrative and exposition are normally interwoven.

The book is divided into three parts. The first is foundational and, therefore, somewhat theoretical, setting out some of the perspectives that should inform community development. It might be tempting to skip over this section and to get on to the more immediately practical issues. But to ignore the groundwork of fundamental principles can mean being oversimplistic and working with un-thought-out assumptions that might not be sustainable in the long run and lead to an ad hoc unstructured pragmatism that can easily lose its way. Not least is this true for the missiological and theological principles that inform Christian practice. While some may engage with the more familiar everyday world first, it is, in the end, essential to return to the undergirding issues that inform practice.

Part II tries to outline some of the key principles of community development. There is no pretence that this is a full introduction to community development as such. For that it is necessary to go to the textbooks and elsewhere. The question that is being asked here is: what does it mean to be the Church in the world as those who are basing their action on the insights and forms of community development?

Part III is about the qualities and strengths and weaknesses of living the Christian life under these perspectives. Central to this is the spirituality and worship both of the individual Christian and the community of faith, rooted in prayer and liturgy.

Each chapter has a bibliography, and these are all to be found together at the end of the book. This enables references to be grouped under topical headings. Of course many books and resources will be relevant under more than one section. While some titles are repeated, this is kept to a minimum. It is necessary, therefore, sometimes to refer to the bibliographies of more than one chapter; but this should not be difficult as it is comparatively easy to spot connections. References are to the edition at hand to the writer, which is normally the latest and not necessarily the original edition. Website addresses are also given for many sources of material or contacts.

Part I

SETTING OUT SOME GUIDELINES

1

The elusive search for community

Community work is 'in'. Both in the welfare world and in the Church a reference to community is a 'good thing'. Thus we have 'living in the community', 'care in the community', 'community groups', 'faith communities' and many more. But only a short pause for reflection shows, first, that the word is being used with many different meanings and, second, that it is being used to slide over the problems and issues that are inherent in the real situation. As too often happens, a 'hooray' concept actually disguises and can oversimplify what it is trying to indicate. So this chapter tries to analyse what is meant by community and what this may imply in practice.

The dilemma

Jim was working on his first annual report. It was not that there was nothing to say. Statistics indicated a growing and thriving enterprise. The question that niggled at the back of his mind was the need to look again at the mission statement for his project. What gave coherence and direction to the disparate and often seemingly disconnected activities? As he thought about it he realized that, at least for his own satisfaction, this pushed him further back. He was a community worker, committed to community development; but what was meant by 'community'? What is the aim? How do we recognize community when we see it?

Jim could recall a valuable conversation with Mary, a senior colleague working out of a secondary school. She had voiced the same question; only she was working in a far tougher locality. Vera, who was with them, however, had dismissed the issue, saying one just got on with the job, instinctively knowing what worked. But for Mary and Jim there had to be some kind of perspective, vision, framework or whatever, that gave a sense of direction to all this activism. They had been appointed to create community, to provide a catalyst for change, as part of a strategy of intervention. This presupposed some sort of need, a pattern of failure that should be rectified or at least mitigated. On what basis was that judgement made? All too often it is assumed that we all know the answer. When, however, the work becomes wearing and disappointing, looking like failure, what sustains the motivation? Moreover there are plenty of sceptics who would argue that it was all a waste of time and that there is no such thing as community, only people living together with greater or lesser success. To have a vision is only to build on a fantasy.

So Jim decides that he has to think this through again. He is beginning to recognize that some of the reading he did in training, which then seemed remote and abstract, is now becoming concrete and relevant. Despite the slipperiness of the notion, the idea of community persists and seems not to be entirely vacuous. Perhaps, on reflection, it may be possible to discern a web of overlapping and related meanings, however tenuous, that gives the concept some coherence. Without it, it would seem difficult to carry on.

A sense of place or relationships?

Why not start where Jim finds himself? He is the community worker on the team of St Ethelburga's Anglican and United Reformed Church and Community Centre in Hurstgate, an inner suburb of a large industrial city. The new, purpose-built centre is there both as a part of the local community and to offer opportunities for creating community. So we have already two uses of the word, the first is about community as place. There are community schools, community hospitals and 'care in the community'. In each case the primary reference is to the neighbourhood.

Hurstgate is a recognizable district. It can be described in terms of boundaries, like the railway and canal, in terms of its facilities, such as the shops and post office, and of its people, from ethnicity to work, from households to age profile. But in what sense is Hurstgate a community? People will certainly identify themselves as coming from Hurstgate, but it is really a very low-key sense of belonging.

People equally and sometimes more strongly identify with other groupings, such as family, culture, interests and status. Nor is that the whole story. These connections run out in all directions. Most people with jobs will commute out of Hurstgate; many will shop in the city centre; and the hospital is across town, as are the cinema complexes and the premier football club. This suggests two things. First, important as geographical locations are, this too is a flexible reality and varies according to what is being considered. For some Hurstgate is the centre of their lives, but for others their spatial location is much wider.

Second, there is a parallel factor in the idea of community: shared interests. One belongs to those groups where people have things in common. But this too is a series of connections that can vary widely from person to person, some intense and treasured, others more functional and occasional. Such relationships may or may not overlap. From any one household its members will relate to a number of other communities, from employment to church, from school to health centre, from the shopping mall to the darts club. Some of these communities transcend the limitations of location. For example, professional people often see themselves primarily as members of a profession that is tied to a place of work. These days there is also the growing acceptance of virtual communities that gather round limited interests.

Even so the importance of place does not go away. The networks that we belong to come together, for us, in our particular location where there has to be some sort of physical proximity and relationship, some kind of human belonging. So in Hurstgate Jim felt that he could see some preliminary shape to the meaning of community. It is clearly many-layered and protean; but it combines a sense of belonging to a place, with others, in a fluctuating, interlocking way. Perhaps the task of community development is to encourage and to enable such a network, both locally and more widely.

The necessity of community

If community is about how people are placed together, is it also true that people need community? Certainly the behavioural psychologists such as Fromm and Maslow have so argued. There is the obvious dependency of the infant on others for sustenance and shelter. Also, starting from birth there is the process of socialization, developing physical, communicative and intellectual abilities. Everyone is thrust into a communal situation of some kind. This persists through to old age and into a second dependency. It is the quality of these relationships that affects their development. So it appears that community is fundamental to flourishing.

Countering this there are two assertions. First, people survive, sometimes remarkably creatively and positively, under what would appear to be very adverse conditions. One has only to think of street kids, of whom it is said that they have 'come through' or 'made good'. Second, and more crucially, cultural patterns down history and across the world have varied so widely and radically it is hard to see any real pattern that can be described as normative for human community.

In reply to this it is possible to offer three considerations. The first is that, though it is true that 'good' experience is not necessary for human survival, it is surely reasonably patent that there are some situations that make for a better quality of life. Love, care, reliability, trust, reciprocity and order make for a happier social experience than, say, hate, fear or anarchy. Second, even in the midst of degradation it is often possible to catch glimpses of the resilience of the human spirit. Loyalty, sacrifice, hope are found flickering in the darkness. Is it possible to suggest that there is an instinctive search for these qualities that can only be described as human? Belief that there is an alternative to the present allows people to 'hang on'. Third, while human societies display an almost infinite variety of cultural patterns, it is also possible to discern some general modes of social existence. For instance, there is always something that can be called a family structure, however many forms it may have taken. There may be no blueprint of what a family is, even in our own society, but there has to be some relationship with 'significant others' who provide succour and support.

What is being asserted here is both a recognition of the difficulty of determining the precise experience and form of community, and the belief that it is possible to see something of a fundamental necessity in human life for something we can only call community. Therefore, there is a need to accept difference and diversity, but also to go on seeking for and discerning true human values in and through that diversity or, perhaps, conflict and deprivation.

The destructive aspects of community

Plant (1974) argues that two dimensions are inextricably joined. Community work has two aims: in the first instance, to develop the quality of community in order to enhance the lives of the individual, and then to assist the self-development of the individual so that each may better contribute to the work of the community. This has a certain circularity; each reinforces the other. At the same time they can work against each other, because community can smother individuality and the individual can be parasitic on community. So there has to be a continuous negotiation if they are to be kept together and not fly apart. At this point consideration needs to be given to some of the negative aspects of community.

First, there is *the issue of boundaries*. Communities are created round collective interests of place, culture, faith, economics or leisure. But that presupposes limits. Boundaries, however, vary in intensity. Some are clear cut, made public by dress or custom, by housing or location. Others are more permeable, such as the Bingo or youth clubs. So recently arrived Somalis are clearly more isolated than a long-standing Irish Catholic community or cosmopolitan young professionals. Boundaries, too, play different roles. A strong sense of core identity will tend to harden them; but so will a sense of threat and fear, driving members to assert their distinctiveness. Zygmunt Bauman (2000) has argued that a strong characteristic of today's society is its extreme individualism that tends to produce great social anxiety. Community, therefore, becomes a defensive measure, securing safety against the chaos. The ultimate form of such community, he avers, is the gated estate. Perhaps one of the reasons why the churches have in recent decades strengthened their public boundaries, which in extreme cases becomes a form of fundamentalism, has been their growing social marginalization. Paradoxically, success, too, can strengthen identities, such as a winning soccer club. On the other hand where a group is at ease, or even dominant, in its setting then separation is less important.

Ironically, just as boundaries are essential to a sense of community, they are equally destructive of community. Hurstgate, as a neighbourhood, would be destroyed if racial riots broke out. Boundaries are where people meet and groups relate. Crossing boundaries is dangerous and open to misinterpretation. Those who do can find themselves mistrusted on both sides. Yet for the wider aspects of community to operate there has to be continuous adjustment and negotiation across boundaries. Perhaps one of the key tasks of community development, both informally and at personal levels, and formally through appropriate structures, is to work along the boundaries so that identities are affirmed and not put under threat and, at the same time, bridges are built, strengthening common interests and action. In any case boundaries are never static. There is always some traffic across them. Groups are forever changing in relation to their environment and responding to opportunities and challenges.

Second, the change from pre-modern society to the ultra-individualism of late- or post-modern society suggests another dynamic of community: *the tension between belonging to a collective and personal freedom*. This can be illustrated from Harvey Cox's *The Secular City* (1965), where he argued that the demise of traditional society is a positive gain. He had escaped from what he saw as the claustrophobic, prescriptive communities of small-town, rural America to the freedom and anonymity of the great metropolis. Bauman, too, suggests that community in the end is restrictive and destructive of human freedom. For Cox full human flourishing is found in the buzz of the city where people's journeys cross and opportunity knocks and boundaries disappear. On the other hand there is a strong evidence that the freedom of the city can mean, for too many, lostness, loneliness and alienation. It is the place of rootlessness and often a sink for the flotsam and jetsam of humanity, a human jungle where the weak are destroyed and only the strong survive. Community in some form is essential as it provides identity and support, a space within which to grow. Community can indeed be destructive but also a lifesaver. Freedom is important but can become a burden. These have to be held in constant tension and dialogue.

The ideology of community

We have, however, also to consider what Plant (1974) calls the 'evaluative' nature of the concept of community (p. 13). It is clearly impossible not to mention the word without it being assumed that it is a 'good thing'. Community is a 'hooray' word. What is happening is that a moral or ideological value is being implied so that the concept, which as we have seen is elusive, is also understood as having a moral imperative behind it. The trouble is that this dimension can seem to answer the question of definition, what community is, whereas it really obscures it. Vagueness of concept is being compensated for by personal or public approbation. The confusion comes to light when the content of any particular sloganistic concept is being unpacked. 'Care in the community' assumes that there is some inherent value in keeping patients in the 'normal' community rather than as inmates of an institution. Does it mean that there is a palpable community there to receive the responsibility for caring, say, for dependent people? Is it an imperative laid on the 'community' which turns out to be family or neighbours? Or is it a way of diffusing responsibility for the cost of care?

Social capital

At this point it is worth introducing an idea that has become currently popular in Government and welfare thinking. The concept of social capital has been recently used by writers such as Robert D. Putnam in debates about civil society to explain the benefits to society that come about when people interact with one another, through the cultivation of goodwill, fellowship, sympathy and social intercourse among those who make up a social unit. So *social capital* refers to the connections between individuals and the benefits that can be brought about by reciprocity, social networking and trust (Putnam 2000, p. 19). It does not take a great deal of imagination to realize that churches can be a useful means by which people support one another to create good (social capital) for society.

Ann Morisy (2004, pp. 45ff.) identifies three kinds of social capital. First there is *bonding social capital*, which is the mutual recognition of those who have common interests of different kinds, whether ethnic, professional, economic or cultural. Here there will be found a strong sense of respect and responsibility, but with the threat that such bonding may be strongly exclusive and restricted. Second, there is *bridging social capital*, that crosses boundaries and builds mutuality between groups. This is a task that is inherent in the gospel, seeking reconciliation between differing, perhaps conflicting, parties. It is also undertaken by those who are engaged in sustaining and creating the wider fabric of society, from race relations to good neighbourliness. *Brave social capital* takes this a step further and works 'for the well-being of those who are not just different, but are perceived as carrying a threat of menace' (Morisy, 2004, p. 61). In other words brave social capital has the ability to go 'the extra mile' at possible personal risk and simply for the sake of those being sought. Society needs a degree of altruism and idealism.

Useful as this terminology can be, it is interesting that in meeting some of the problems associated with a concern for community, many of the same questions come up. There is a tendency to think that the issue is solved simply by coining a term. There is still the problem of actually identifying the good that is supposed to be there for the benefit of the social fabric and the woman and man in the street. Once again there is a conflation of description and value.

This relation between value and experience has been a perennial issue for moral philosophy. For many an absolute distinction has to be made between what is and what ought to be the case. It is impossible to deduce what ought to be done from the given situation. Clearly this has to be taken seriously. It is too easy to introduce evaluative assumptions into one's practice. There may be a number of ideological views offered as explanations for a situation. So, to return to Hurstgate, the presence of a number of ethnic groups did not imply any particular notion of how best to be a multicultural society. What is needed is continuous debate and the search for common ground that engenders mutual respect and openness which can lead to acceptable common patterns. But even to say that is to be ideologically influenced.

Is, however, such a dichotomy between fact and value as absolute as all that? We are constantly using concepts that carry both descriptive and evaluative connotations: for instance, family or democracy. This suggests that, despite the pitfalls, we do in fact see a connection between what is there and the demands this imposes. This is never, however, a straightforward solution. While we cannot jump from what is there to what ought to be done, what is the fact of the case will inform what should be done. Abject poverty, in and of itself, does not require any action. What stimulates action is a belief in the wrongness of allowing people to live in wretchedness. But such a belief is given support from a number of facts, such as that we would not want to live in such conditions and that poverty can lead to violence and disruptive behaviour. The concept of community is of such a kind. It is recognized as a good because, however difficult to describe, it seems to lead to human flourishing.

Christian perspectives on community

For Jim, personally and as a member of the ministerial team at St Ethelburga's, these ideological and moral considerations were also rooted in Christian faith. For him it was important that a Christian understanding of community and community work was not simply a kind of 'faith icing', decorating and confirming what had been arrived at by other means. Of course church-related community work operates in the same context as other community work and will use the same tools of social analysis and practical skills. It will also be done alongside others with different convictions, but is happy to collaborate in various projects. The explicit theological emphasis may often be kept in the background. But those engaged in Christian community work should themselves appropriate the resources of their tradition so that it becomes the normative foundation for thought and practice. Then, when appropriate, it is possible to 'give account of the hope' that is there undergirding their involvement (1 Peter 3.15).

Indeed it was necessary in the light of the considerations that Jim had just been reviewing. So he reconsidered a number of biblical and theological themes that had long given him a framework for his work. He could also learn much from what other traditions (e.g. the Catholics) value.

The fundamental theological perspective on the human condition is that the universe, in all its vastness and evolving mystery, is created. Marvellously, that included this corner of the cosmos that we call home. And in this immensity, whether alone or not, humankind is created in the image of God (Genesis 1. 26–27). Such an assertion carries with it four implications.

First, we are responsible to God as well as to each other for the use that is made of the resources of the world. For good or ill, collectively and individually, human beings have power and it matters how that is exercised, for flourishing or for destruction.

Second, everything is gift. Nothing exists as of right but is given the light of day and the rest of night. Therefore all things are precious, gifts to us, that, however obscurely, enrich our lives. This is more obviously true of those who are our neighbours, but is equally true of those who, unseen to us, share with us in the web of exchange and responsibility. And this gratitude spills out over the whole of creation.

Third, human existence is fundamentally relational. We exist only as family, neighbours, colleagues, 'tribes and tongues', as we participate in the social and economic structures, both contributing and receiving. Thus community, whatever it is, and in its various forms and expressions, is part of the very fabric of our existence.

Fourth, this is rooted in the very nature of God. The Christian understanding of God as Trinity – three persons in one godhead –

puts community at the heart of the universe. All language about God is partial and inadequate. Yet Christians want to affirm that the threefold experience of God – as the transcendent yet benevolent creator; as revelation, the living historical presence and sacrament of the divine in humanity; as sustainer, the mystical presence in the midst of our existence – truly reflects the divine reality in itself. These three are one so that there is perfect unity. Yet the unity does not destroy the diversity; nor does the diversity shatter the unity. Here is a model for community that differentiates in togetherness and yet finds harmony in and through their particularities.

It is patent, however, that the human condition is fragmented and constantly under threat. The Christian doctrine of sin suggests that an essential ambiguity exists in all human action. The good is always corrupted, dragged down or misappropriated. Yet it is never entirely lost and is often found in surprising places. There is always a sense of longing and striving for the better. Even the addict, fleeing from reality, is saying that there can be something better. The good is often tainted and distorted. We easily mistake where it can be found, are tempted to find it through short cuts, or seize it for our selfish ends, or fail to understand its true nature. Yet there are also many and various reasons to be thankful. Thus there is always hope: evil cannot be shrugged off easily, but it is not the last word. 'The light shines in the darkness, and the darkness did not overcome it' (John 1.5).

This points to a vision – the Kingdom of God. This is what Christians pray for ceaselessly. 'Your Kingdom come. Your will be done, on earth as it is in heaven' (Matthew 6.10, NRSV). That is, the harmony of God's intention can and will be manifested on earth. It is in part as people and communities begin to live in the mode of that prayer, relying on God, finding and giving forgiveness and seeking to resist the destructiveness of evil, that the Kingdom starts to take root, the Kingdom that Jesus enacted and into which he calls us to enter while waiting for its consummation.

Perhaps the most potent symbol of this Kingdom is peace – *shalom*. There is an image, found in the Hebrew Scriptures: 'They shall all sit under their own vines and under their own fig trees'

(Micah 4.4; cf. Zechariah 3.10). Householders are safe with their families and at peace with their neighbours. Prosperity is assured. Under the fig tree one can meditate and give thanks. Peace, therefore, is not tranquillity but a network of relationships that bind together a community in justice and mutuality, the participants embracing each other in trust, respect and affection, sharing the joy and responsibility of a common life. This is well summed up in Psalm 85.10–13.

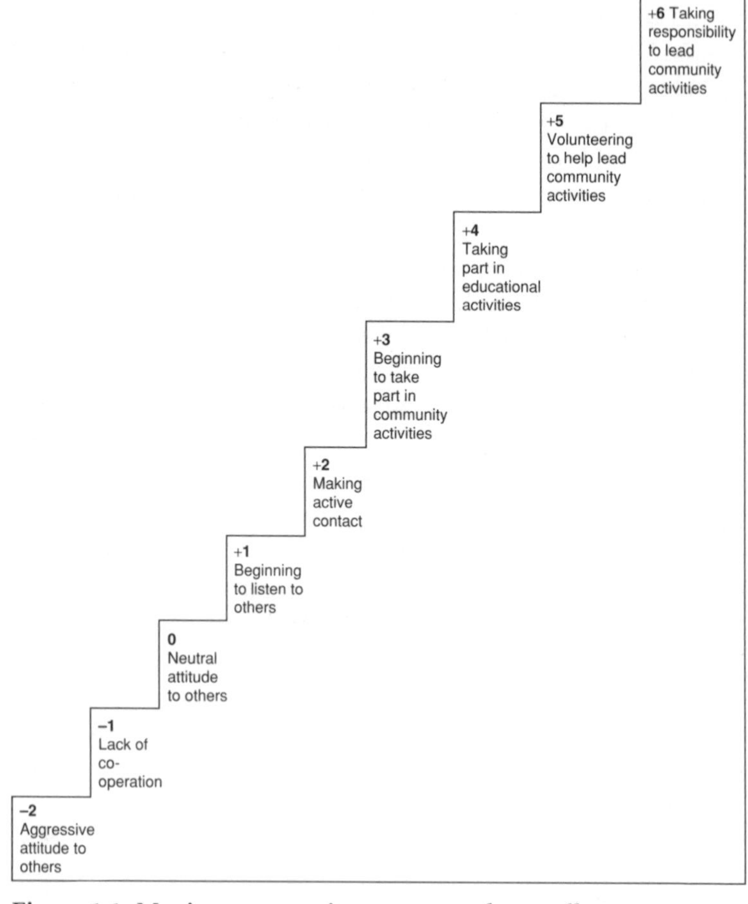

Figure 1.1 Moving community groups on by small steps

L. Husselbee. Adapted from: *Straat voor straat. Delphi Opbouwwerk. Door straataanpak meer sociale binding*, December 2004 © Delphi Opbouwwerk, Vermijding Stichting Delphi Opbouwwerk Rotterdam Delfshaven, Havenstraat 183, 3024 SK Rotterdam p. 13.

Jim's final image is that of the accompanying presence. This is in some ways the most difficult to imagine and, certainly, to describe. Yet in some ways it is the most important. It is the promise that we are not alone. Nor in a sense are we ultimately responsible. The only demand is that we be faithful; and even then there is one to pick us up in the failures that are our human lot. At the same time there is the belief that in the limited and hesitant ways that we are able to contribute to the welfare of the community, it is possible to tap into the pulse of the universe; and that we share in this with all that makes for healing and joy and peace. If, thought Jim, I see the flower of peace blossom, even if only in a glimpse and in harsh and unforgiving conditions from time to time, then the work is not in vain.

Meanwhile his understanding of community had been enlarged. More importantly community workers have to recognize the significance of the vision that underlies their motivations, and keeps them going in and through the business of their activism. He and other colleagues, Jim realizes, are not going to make much of an impact very quickly. Progress may often appear to be very slow or non-existent; but it is often the case that small improvements have been made. The work progresses incrementally, a step at a time. It may also be that it starts from a very low base. What is important is to be facing in the right direction. This is set out in Figure 1.1. If there is any movement upwards, starting at any point, then something of what community implies has been achieved. Reflecting on the work done can often demonstrate that a project has made progress, even if it is in small steps.

2

Community work and mission

Most congregations recognize that mission includes working in, for and with the wider community. But that is not the whole of mission, for mission also includes making disciples and drawing people into the pilgrimage of faith. There seems, however, to be a tension here between offering unconditional love and care and calling others into the life of the gospel. This is a tension that is at the heart of Christian witness, and it has to be understood and worked through and lived with in practice.

The challenge of Market Street

Susan had just been called as pastor of Market Street United Free Church in the centre of Springtown, a smallish country town which was both the commercial and retail centre for the surrounding area and a dormitory for the nearby metropolitan area. The town centre, where Market Street was to be found, was a shopping precinct and office district, including the Town Hall. So the town centre was busy during weekdays and at weekends was a focus for those, mostly young, who wanted to have a drink, eat out, go to the cinema or occasional concert, or just hang out. Part of her brief had been to explore how the church should develop its ministry. To this end the church had set up a small working party.

Susan, however, had also brought with her a commitment to a part-time MA in Practical Theology, in a university department in the nearby city. This was demanding and required a disciplined use of time; but it was also rewarding as it allowed her to reflect on her ministry and the issues that confronted her. The current assignment on perspectives on mission was precisely appropriate for her present task. She could get to grips with aspects of missiological thinking that would give her a theological handle on the situation and, perhaps as important as anything, resources to enable the people of Market Street Church to see the possibly radical changes they were going to face.

Susan found herself drawing together three kinds of material. There was, first of all, the cumulative information gathered from her expanding range of contacts in the shops and offices, including the statutory agencies, as well as the pubs and clubs and other places of entertainment. This supplemented the work of the church's working party. Second, Susan was grateful for the ministers' fellowship of the Churches Together group. This opened up relationships with other congregations, not least the parish church on the Market Square; but it also meant that she could tap into the experience and wisdom of colleagues. Then, third, there were the books. These provided the broad systematic background, challenging questions and sometimes surprising insights. What she wanted out of her academic assignment was a clarification of the issues and an idea of the range of possible theological and missiological responses.

The wholeness of mission

In order to understand the possibilities open to the congregation and to be able to evaluate the range of options so that a policy could emerge it is necessary to have a firm grasp of the nature of the Church and its mission. So Susan had to place the question of Market Street's challenge to greater social involvement against a mission perspective.

Modern missiology starts from the mystery of God and an understanding of God's cosmic purposes. This is encapsulated in the phrase *missio Dei*, mission of God. The Christian belief is in the God who is essentially a sending God, one who reaches out for the good of all creation. It points, therefore, in two directions. It takes us first into the ineffable reality of God as Trinity and the creative depth of love in the perfect communion of Father, Son and Spirit, a love that spills out into the wonders of creation without limit and without end; out into the universe in all its vastness and splendour, cast into the dangers and risks of time and space, as an expression of God's restless yearning for the glory of the creature. This God also wills to be in and with the creature in ways that are beyond comprehension. For us this is the intimacy that is vouchsafed to us in and through the incarnate reality of Jesus as the Christ and through the living presence of the Spirit. So the *missio Dei* faces out from God towards the cosmos and informs its direction and purpose. In ways that we can never know, though we are discovering more and more of the wonders of creation, all things are caught up into the love of God who wills its good and in whom it finds its fulfilment. Nothing is outside the sweep of God's action. For us this is demonstrated and defined in the reality of Christ who is the historical manifestation of the cosmic reality.

Such a majestic theme beats as a constant rhythm in the New Testament. Witness the sweep of 1 Corinthians 15.12–28, ending with 'God will be all in all'. Or the ringing tone of Romans 8.18–36 where the Apostle sees us caught up into the story of creation. Or John's hymn to the Word by whom all things came into existence (John 1.1–14.).

There does indeed seem to be something new here, or at least a recovery in a fresh way, of a dimension previously underplayed. David Bosch (1991) sees this as part of a 'paradigm shift', or change of direction, that emerged in the mid twentieth century from the earlier Protestant and Enlightenment eras of mission. Those saw the emphasis in mission in terms of salvation, especially personal salvation. Mission was the Church's witness to the redeeming acts of God in Christ and the calling of people to faith. Of course there was a concern for the quality of people's lives but this tended to be individualized and secondary to the essential dimension of the gospel. Such a model is still very much present, not least in the so-called conservative churches. The more recent model, however, shifts the emphasis from the Church to the cosmic will of God for all creation. This does not make the Church superfluous or air-brush it out of the picture, but refocuses it as the witness to and an instrument of the fuller *missio Dei*. Nor does it destroy the need for calling people to faith. The Christian understanding of what makes the world tick must include, in its fullness, a recognition of God's creating, saving and accompanying love.

Faith, as grateful reassurance, is both the final reality of who we are and the trust in the one who takes us along the journey into that ultimate reality we call God.

Susan would be right to see that this cosmic vision impacts directly on the challenges and opportunities of the immediate present. First, it broadens the perception of what the gospel is about. It includes all levels of our existence, from the personal to the communal, from the private to the public, and from the 'spiritual' to the mundane. So, second, the gospel is about the here and now as much as the hereafter. While the Kingdom of God, in all its fullness, may be in the future and something we pray for, it also is, at least in anticipation, present where there is true worth found in people's lives. God has placed us in our actual situation precisely to witness to and be part of the striving for the Kingdom, however limited our scope. John V. Taylor expressed it thus:

> Mission, therefore, means to recognise what the Creator-Redeemer is doing in the world and to try to do it with him . . . We can see now the enormous breadth and range of the mission of the Creator Spirit . . . The missionaries of the Holy Spirit include the probation officer and the literary worker, the research chemist and the worn out school teacher in a remote village, the psychiatrist and the designer, the famine relief worker and the computer operator, the pastor and the astronaut. (Taylor, 1972, pp. 37–38)

Susan could add the patient housewife and mother, the single parent doing her best for her child, the shopkeeper or builder, the civil servant, doctor and policeman. From another, rather different source, Gustavo Gutiérrez, the father of Latin American liberation theology, writes:

> When we assert that man fulfils himself by continuing the work of creation by means of his labour, we are saying that he places himself, by this very fact, within the all-embracing salvific process. To work to transform this world, is to become a man and to build the human community; it is also to save. Likewise, to struggle against misery and

exploitation and to build a just society is already to be part of the saving action which is moving towards its complete fulfilment. (Gutiérrez, 1974, p. 159)

Witness and service

These considerations open up, however, the longstanding debate about the relationship between proclamation and service. This was sharply characterized in the clash between the World Council of Churches (WCC) and many leading evangelicals in the 1960s. It was averred that the ecumenical movement had obscured, even done away with, the focal mandate of the Church to 'make disciples' (Matthew 28.28) in favour of a gospel of social development. This came to a climax at the 1968 WCC Assembly in Uppsala where mission was clearly talked of in terms of *shalom* or 'humanization'. The implication was that 'the world must be allowed to provide the agenda for the churches' as much as it was the Christian task to 'recognise and proclaim what God was doing in the world' (WCC Report, 1967, quoted in Bosch 1991, p. 383). Evangelism, as the call to repentance and faith, had seemingly disappeared, though a careful look would show that this dimension was always present in WCC thinking. This impression was reinforced by the widespread embrace, in ecumenical circles, of liberation theology and its radical concerns for economic justice and human rights.

Over against this, influential evangelical voices were heard in protest, demanding a clear reaffirmation of the need to proclaim Christ as Saviour and the saving need for faith. This came out at the 1974 Lausanne Congress, which produced a definitive statement of the evangelical position in the form of a Covenant (see Scherer and Bevans 1992). Clause 4 set out 'the nature of evangelism': 'Evangelism itself is the proclamation of the historical, biblical Christ as Saviour (1 Co. 1:23; 2 Co. 4:5) and Lord, with a view to persuading people to come to him personally and so be reconciled to God (2 Co. 5:11, 20).' This was not conceived narrowly, for it also recognized the need for contextualization and a proper dialogue of understanding as well as the realities of Christian discipleship. It was not possible, however, even then, to deny the centrality of 'Christian social responsibility' (clause 5). God demands justice and liberation from oppression. Every person has the rights of one who is made in God's image.

> Although reconciliation with other people is not reconciliation with God, nor is social action evangelism, nor political liberation salvation, nevertheless we affirm that evangelism and socio-political involvement are both part of our Christian duty. For both are necessary expressions of our doctrines of God and man, our love for our neighbour and our obedience to Christ. (Clause 5)

Immediately it can be seen that there is not the absolute contrast between these two strands that some would want to insist. In point of fact it has been widely noted that there has subsequently been a real convergence, though both sides represent wide constituencies of great diversity. Thus the WCC in its 1982 *Ecumenical Affirmation: Mission and Evangelism* (see Scherer and Bevans 1992) set out the shared understanding in a series of 'Convictions', the first of which was 'Conversion': 'The proclamation of the Gospel includes an invitation to recognise and accept in a personal decision the saving lordship of Christ' (para. 10).

At the same time the evangelicals have more and more strongly reappropriated their own tradition of radical social concern and have themselves been influenced by the cries for liberation and justice from the Southern Hemisphere. So in the *Manila Manifesto* (1989) there appears, *inter alia*,

> Jesus not only proclaimed the Kingdom of God, he also demonstrated its arrival by works of mercy and power (Mt. 12:28). We are called today to similar integration of words and deeds (1 Jn. 3:18). . . . The proclamation of God's kingdom necessarily demands prophetic denunciation (Jer. 22:1–5, 11–17; 23:5–6) of all that is incompatible with it . . . Our continuing commitment to social action is not a confusion of the Kingdom of God with a Christianised society. It is, rather, a recognition that the biblical gospel has inescapable social implications (Eph. 2:8–10). True mission

> should always be incarnational (Jn. 17:18; 20:21). (clause 4) (see Scherer and Bevans 1992)

There is, however, a third strand in this convergence. Pope Paul VI, in *Evangelii Nuntiandi* (1975), set out afresh the Catholic teaching on mission, continuing the work of Vatican II as set out in *Ad Gentes*.

> Evangelism is in fact the grace and vocation proper to the Church in her deepest identity . . . But evangelization would not be complete if it did not take account of the necessary interplay of the Gospel and of man's concrete life, both personal and social. (*Evang. Nun.* 14 and 29; see Scherer and Bevans 1992)

There is a hint in those words, however, of a different way of thinking from the sometimes stark contrast made between evangelism and social concern among Protestants. Evangelism, in the Catholic tradition, is a continuing process. The gospel calls all humankind into a saving relationship with God, a call that is continually needed as we are brought further into the gracious will of God. In other words, conversion is only complete at the end, when all things, including the Church, are brought into the final Kingdom. This is close to the concept of *missio Dei*. There does not, however, seem to be a necessary tension between the two uses of evangelism. Both point to an essential and compatible truth. Evangelism is, indeed, the call to faith and that always has to be present, but we constantly need to be recalled to the basics of the gospel in order to grow in Christ.

Models of community work in mission

Drawing on the fuller tradition had meant that the people of Market Street Church saw themselves as part of a wider scene that encompassed the world. It had raised them from being obsessed with their own difficulties of decline and change. It was possible to underline the fact that the congregation was already embedded in the local community through the everyday life of its members and the activities of the church. Many, too, were found in a wide variety of voluntary service. Yet even so there was still need to define more closely what it meant to embrace community activities as part of their mission. A bland endorsement was not enough. It is to this that Susan now has to turn.

A way forward may be to look again at the tension between evangelism, in the narrow sense of proclamation, and social concern, in the form of community-related activity. Given the earlier discussion there seem to be four ways of defining this relationship.

Social engagement arising from evangelism

First, social engagement can be seen as consequent upon evangelism. The primary task of the Church is to proclaim the gospel. Out of the transforming power of the gospel comes the desire both to witness to it by the quality of life of the individual and of the fellowship of the Church; and to be involved in caring for the neighbour and the community through acts of compassion. This has been the motivation behind much, often heroic, endeavour. Laws have been changed, foundations set up, education provided and hospitals built. It is true that faith should lead to action. It still, however, plays down the importance of the present world and does not reflect the fullness of the Kingdom. There would have to be a stronger grounding than this if social concern is to be integral to the witness of the Church.

Social engagement as evangelism

Second, social engagement can be seen as an essential aspect of evangelism. The love of God for humanity has to be proclaimed in both word and deed. A genuine Christian concern for others and the life of the community exhibits and mediates God's seeking to give fullness of life. Word without deed is abstract; but deed without word is anonymous (cf. James 2.18). As in the sacraments, community concern is enacted Word, yet needs the Word to be spoken, or at least explicit, for it to be a complete witness. Thus in the context of social concern the source and aim of the caring is explicit, the redeeming work of Christ.

At its best this indicates a real concern for those around and a full recognition of their freedom and worth. Indeed it is a part of the gospel that God loves and respects each and everyone. It is better to be up front about the basic stance rather than try, by avoiding 'naming the name', not to cause stumbling, and to win respect through the integrity and quality of the service offered. Nor does this mean being overly 'in your face' with the Christian dimension. This is best built into the culture of acceptance and friendliness, even while being clear that faith is the undergirding reality.

Susan is fully aware of the thriving community centre, which is highly thought of, in the Brethren Hall on the edge of town. This runs all manner of programmes but maintains an explicitly Christian ethos and is base for activities such as a Christian counselling centre, openly accessible to all. However, there are some real questions to be asked about this model. Some would argue that, in a secular society, to be so overtly Christian can be unnecessarily off-putting. Others, more crucially, would cite the case of 'rice Christians', those who appear to accept the religious bit for the sake of the other benefits. Susan remembered a tutor in college telling of how, in his student days, as an assignment, he was expected to preach to the down-and-outs under the railway arches, for whom this was the price of the bread and soup provided for them. This did not mean that nothing good ever came out of it, but it felt like a betrayal of the gospel. There are also issues of ownership. There is a tendency to think of service as from those who have to those who have not. At the same time, some kind of control has to be maintained in order to ensure that the fundamental aims of the project are sustained. So, however desirable, client participation and ownership is difficult to manage unless there is agreement with the terms laid down by the initiating authority. Again Susan could remember from her teenage years how in the church youth club every decision had to be referred to the Elders lest they breach some accepted norms.

Evangelism and social concern in parallel

Third, evangelism and social concern are seen as two parallel expressions of the mission of the Kingdom. This has the advantage of giving community work its own integrity. The quality of human life is God's concern at each and every point. People and their communities have their own worth. Any project run by or from the Church is a gift and a contribution to the common good and the community at large. It underlines the servant role of the Church which is in the world, as William Temple is reported to have once said, 'for the benefit of those who are not its members'. There are no strings attached. The aim is not to win converts, though such will be welcomed as and when they appear. Rootedness in the gospel is not denied and people can ask whence comes this concern; but that is not the primary aim. True to community development principles, the stress is on the participants and their needs, seeking to enable them to take greater responsibility for their own activities. Ownership, therefore, can be primarily with the project and those involved. Susan had an example of this in the Methodist church down by the station where their old church buildings had been converted to community use, and where all manner of activities took place reflecting the needs of that poorer end of town.

That very example, however, she found, exhibited some of the possible problems with this model. It was apparent that the congregation and the community project had drawn apart. There were two parallel sets of activities operating side by side. For the congregation, largely drawn from a wider area than the immediate locality, and the minister, who had inherited but not set up the situation, the community activities were something that went on in the building and were even occasionally a nuisance. By the same token, for those using the building the fact that it was a church with a congregation was incidental. The church was simply a landlord. Only very occasionally were the connections overtly recognized. Such a situation is all too common. But this obscures the basic gospel motivation. If the two strands are to run side by side then there is a real onus on the Christian congregation to ensure that their vision is sustained and to find ways of owning, accepting and contributing to the community activities while at the same time allowing them true freedom and autonomy. This 'hidden discipline', to borrow a phrase from Dietrich Bonhoeffer, has to be woven into the very spirituality of the congregation (Bonhoeffer 1967, p. 281).

Community concern at the centre

The fourth model inverts the second model by putting community concern at the centre and making the life of faith incidental. This may well be one of the ways that some will want to express their self-understanding. Susan had heard of an example of an inner-city church in a multicultural area which had turned its premises over completely to community use, setting up an association to control and manage the building. The congregation had then simply become one of the users, working alongside the rest. Another possible parallel Susan could think of was the parish church in a nearby village which participated in the local carnival as one of the village organizations, contributing its own float to the annual procession. Here the Church is but one voluntary organization among many. Its special distinctive contribution to the wider community is simply to represent the possibility of a spiritual dimension, which people may or may not want to take up if 'they like that sort of thing'. This may include a wide range of activities from worship, through the occasional offices associated with birth, family and death, to educational, counselling or fellowship groups. The heart of the matter, however, is the common life of the community.

Such a pattern would seem to reflect acutely the secular reality of contemporary culture and the marginalization of the Church. There are, of course, examples of Christian communities that turn their back on the wider life of society, such as the closed Brethren and some communes. But to allow oneself to be pushed into a ghetto is to negate God's concern and power in and for the world. At the present time, however, this may seem to be what is happening in practice. It is hard to witness to the concerns of the Kingdom in a cold cultural climate, even though there are signs that this is changing. Yet surely even in the two examples Susan had recalled there was still a desire to connect with what counted in those communities.

Some other recent developments

Two new approaches, which are better seen as variants on the classical discussion, have emerged in the post-Christian context in which we find ourselves. First, it has long been recognized in church growth theory (McGavran 1959) that evangelism, in the sense of an expanding church, is most effective through homogeneous cultural units; that is, faith is transmitted more readily among those who share common social values. So social structures provide the opportunities for mission, which is very likely also to include social concerns. In British society, for example, the Catholic community has traditionally supported a considerable network of charitable activity among its own people. In post-Christian western society, not least in the urban context, new churches have been emerging that relate to the changing social patterns in society. Some, for instance, are associated with ethnic minority and immigrant groups, such as the black-led churches. These, too, often provide educational and welfare services. Other emerging churches, often smaller and experimental, relate to patterns of living or working, from the inner-city to professional groups or the new city-centre residential communities, sometimes stemming out of felt social need.

The other also relates to the post-Christian or postmodern scene and the growing reference to 'faith communities' which recognizes that the Church is but one religious tradition among many in a secular society. A positive assessment of this situation argues that the churches, which have been too closely assimilated into Enlightenment modernism and have thereby lost their distinctive voice, are now free to rediscover their heritage. The Church is a public body in an open society whose task it is to serve the body politic, offering by proclamation, debate and service an alternative way of seeing the world. It is not yet too clear what this might mean in terms of social witness in the local congregation, though some, for instance, have become actively involved in faith-based schooling, or holistic health clinics and Christian counselling centres of differing kinds. At another more general level this perspective can be seen in the desire to reinvigorate 'public theology', finding ways to enter into the debates concerning the direction of national life. Practically this is reflected in the participation of Christian groups in the Government's interest in increasing the participation of the 'voluntary sector' as 'partners' in the delivery of some social and educational services.

These then are the four major patterns for the relationship between witness and service. They are each able to be broadly construed and they are obviously by no means necessarily mutually incompatible and to some extent merge into one another; but this is not to minimize some of the tensions between them. The nub of the problem is in holding together, creatively and sensitively, the desire of the members of the church at Market Street to work in and with the community as part of their commitment and witness to the love of God, and the expectations and assumptions and perhaps the indifference and incomprehension of a dominantly secular culture. This interface itself is not, however, a simple issue but one complicated by a number of different attitudes and possibilities.

Responding to the world's agenda

Susan found three sets of differing attitudes among those with whom she came in contact in the wider community.

At one level there was a real suspicion of the Church, with the assumption that there was an inherent inappropriateness in the Church 'interfering' in matters beyond its competence. For some there had been 'bad' experiences in time past which had been off-putting. Others wondered what the Church was going to get out of it. Was it just a way to proselytize? In any case religion did not mix with public or commercial activities. Occasionally there was a clear anti-religious attitude. So there was a barrier that ranged from indifference to antagonism.

Alongside this and surprisingly frequently, there was a welcome for the Church's interest. As she got to know the stallholders and staff in some of the shops and offices there was often a warm reception. 'Where have you been all this time?' 'It is about time the Church took us seriously!' 'We need someone like you around.' And she began to forge what were pastoral connections, including the possibility of a store chaplaincy. There was considerable support for the Christmas and harvest celebrations at the midweek lunch-hour service and there was an interest in the possibility of the church being more widely used for community activities.

Susan was also encouraged by the ready welcome given to her by the relevant council departments. This reflected the policy, to which the Government has been giving the lead, of involving the voluntary sector in matters of welfare and social capital. The so-called 'faith communities' have a high priority. This is seen as a way of building cross-cultural contacts and strengthening the welfare provision for the members of those communities, but also a way of encouraging them to contribute to the common good. Such activities, however, too often have to be as far as possible 'faith neutral'. This poses a dilemma as to whether such collaboration is unnecessarily restrictive of freedom for the churches. Sometimes it seems like being accepted for what the Church can give towards an already agreed agenda.

It is proper that the Christian community should be engaged in the concerns and needs of the society they are in. Indeed, the Church and its members are part of that wider society. But it is equally important that sight is not lost of the particular gifts that the churches bring to the common good of wisdom and tradition. The William Temple Foundation's recent study (Baker and Skinner 2006) has valuably discerned two elements that are intrinsic to the churches as faith communities. Alongside social capital it is proposed to set 'religious capital' and 'spiritual capital'. Religious capital consists in 'the practical contribution to local and national life made by faith groups'. This ranges from the corporate life of the church itself to its being an asset for the wider community through buildings and projects. Spiritual capital is the beliefs, values and practices that inform and create the faith community; that is 'what makes it tick'. It is this double heritage that the Church has to cultivate if it is to be the Church and make its contribution to the common good. Perhaps the problem presently is finding ways of being the Church.

All this had to be taken into account when formulating the policy that would inform any new developments that Market Street would seek to pursue. How far were they to be overt about their Christian foundations? How far could they co-operate with other agencies, voluntary or statutory? Or was it to be a mix, the management and policies of any part of the project being appropriate for that initiative without prejudice to the rest? This latter would be harder to work with but potentially richer and allowing for greater diversity. Whichever way they went, it would always be essential that the whole programme, whatever it turned out to be, was owned and supported by the congregation as a whole. It must be accepted as a real example of the pluriform expression of mission which is serving the creative and saving activities of God.

Thus, Susan insisted that discussions be more than looking at the practical possibilities identified by the working party, but should include reflection on what was at stake in faith terms. So a series of consultations was set up, which enabled them to hear other people's stories, to study the Bible and to discuss what this all meant in terms of mission. Out of it came an agreed statement which was accepted by the church as a whole and which would become the template by which all actions would be measured and reviewed annually. As things developed, all the activities were seen to be woven into a complex and delicate pattern through which a number of different threads ran, each contributing to the whole vision. Depending where one was placed at any given moment, some of the colours dominated while others were less visible, but still part of the pattern. But there was a consistency which included faith in God, service in and with Christ, the recognition of the Spirit's work at every point of life, and responsibility for the good of the society in which we live. For those who can see, it is the warp and woof of God's creative grace that holds it together, a pattern that is inclusive and open, being woven continuously into ever new variations.

The congregation in effect found itself in the tension between the second and third models of the relation between evangelism and service. As a church, its engagement with the wider community was an expression of the members' faith and of God's desire for the fullness of life that can be found in Christ. They do it for Jesus' sake. Yet they do it for the other's sake, for the sake of the community, without strings attached. They do not want to hide their identity as a Christian fellowship, nor deny that they want to share their faith. Yet their concern is for the welfare of the neighbour, openly and freely expressed. It is not always easy to know when one can or should shift from one emphasis to the other. It is a pragmatic tension, a tension of human limitation and incompleteness. Amazingly it is a tension in God who wants the best for his creatures. God saves in love and love draws the beloved, yet does not compel. As Christians we are ourselves subject to that tension, for we are not yet complete, and have to work within it in our service as those who are Christ's ambassadors. Only when all things come together in Christ in God's Kingdom will the tension be resolved.

3

Models and modes of community work

There are almost as many ways of doing community work as there are understandings of community and styles of Christian mission. It is important, therefore, to recognize some of the main patterns of approach that are to be found in community work and to achieve some clarity as to the basic principles involved and how one wants to work.

There would seem to be three areas for discussion. First there are the principles that inform the recognized modes of community work. Then there are the models found in community work practice. Lastly these have to be thought through theologically in order to discern the key Christian perspectives that ought to be undergirding church-related community work.

Models of community work

Sometimes discussions, not least in church circles, about how to go about community work can go round and round, getting nowhere. Often this is because there are clashing points of view and unacknowledged assumptions knocking around. Once these are out in the open there is a greater chance both of discerning which values to espouse and of coming to a working agreement. Moreover, where projects are set up without a real attempt to clarify these issues, while they may work well, when there is a crisis demanding sensitive judgement it may be found that there is a time bomb ticking away. It is therefore always worth while spending time to have some clarity as to the principles from which any given group works.

Generally speaking it is possible to discern three key approaches to community work: community service, community development and community action. Each approach has its strengths and weaknesses and each can be embodied in a wide variety of different patterns of practice. Nor are the models necessarily mutually exclusive, and they may be found together informing a single situation. They often interlink and, in the changes that affect any situation, there can be movement from one to the other.

Community service

The first is community service or community provision, whereby an organization or project is created to 'meet the needs of the community'. If community work can be described as action taken to break the cycle of deprivation or disadvantage, community service is intervention, undertaken by those who have the authority or resources or power, acting on behalf of the needy or wider society.

Historically this has been the classic expression of community work. The great philanthropists who tried to mitigate the worst excesses of the Industrial Revolution were motivated by a deep sense of responsibility to those who were powerless and a compassion for their suffering; they include such as Elizabeth Fry, Lord Shaftesbury and Dr Barnardo. From this came a wealth of institutions, from poor schools, including the Sunday School, settlements in slum districts and orphanages. A civic pride also was found in the new cities that provided for its people water, transport and hospitals. This is also the foundation for the Welfare State. Out of the experience of the Second World War came the desire to slay Lord Beveridge's five giants: want, disease, ignorance, squalor and idleness. This meant universal state intervention which spawned new or enlarged professional groups. It is clearly an honourable tradition which properly persists, and probably dominates thinking among congregations thinking about service in the community.

Reflection, however, would suggest that there is a certain dynamic underlying community work conceived of in this way. It is essentially interventionist, coming into a situation from outside in order to bring about change. That would imply that the following elements are more or less characteristic of community service.

1 The cycle of deprivation, injustice or disadvantage has to be broken from outside. There are little or no resources from within. At its worst this can lead to the assumption that those at the bottom of society are weak and even may have brought their plight on themselves.
2 Poverty and deprivation are an expression of a failure in the system but can be controlled and corrected by the system if the necessary adjustments are made or the abuses eradicated.
3 Power and authority are outside the point of need. Much research and thought can go into identifying the actual need and the appropriate response, with great care taken to work in partnership with those being served. However, in the end, the buck stops with the provider of the resources. This has become even more acute in an era when 'value for money' is paramount and accountability a core virtue. Indeed there may be several layers of accountability, distancing the point of decision ever more from the point of delivery. Monitoring can have the effect of making those operating a scheme or project more anxious to satisfy the regulator than respond to the needs of the client.
4 Resources come from outside. A culture of dependency can therefore emerge. This may be expressed in an unwillingness to take responsibility, and a readiness to allow the provider to do all the work. At its worst there can be an assumption that others are there to satisfy certain needs.
5 There can be a stress on expertise and professional competence. This again places power and authority in the hands of the provider, playing down the competence of the volunteer or the resources to be found in the disadvantaged community.
6 Thus, often subtly, it is the attitudes and perspective of those outside that govern the situation. While there is indeed a real empathy for the client and shared expectations, there is the very real possibility of imposing presuppositions and decisions that are actually based on external considerations, moulding others into an alien pattern.

Community service is sometimes summarized as *working for people* rather than working *with* them. There are clear dangers. It can degenerate into and earn the reputation of being 'do-goodery' or 'lady bountiful'. It can leave the client feeling marginalized and patronized. Yet it is a tradition that, as we have seen, has had a rich history and should not be dismissed out of hand. The resources of society, including its wealth and expertise, should be at the service of the vulnerable and disadvantaged. There is a valuable tradition that sees power and wealth as responsibility, to be used for the welfare of all and especially the protection of the weak. People should feel that there is value and dignity in being part of the welfare system and its delivery. There is a reservoir of good will and altruism that can be properly channelled. Society must be inclusive. And, indeed, it may be that it is only by intervention that a situation can, at least in the first instance, be met adequately or creatively, or those in need be enabled to begin to break out of the vicious cycle in which they find themselves.

Community development

Community development is usually characterized, in contrast to community service, as *working with people* instead of *for* them. It, too, has a credible history. Modern community development is rooted in colonial history. In order to enhance the life of the people, especially in the rural villages, self-help local projects were stimulated. The people would then develop the skills and devise the means to put them into operation, whether it be on a well or land drainage, crop diversification or a school. External resources and skills would be available in relation to those needs and there to enable the local community to become independent. This continues to be a significant model for development work, not least among church agencies such as CAFOD, Tearfund and Christian Aid. The slogan is familiar: 'Give a man a fish and he is fed for a day; teach a man to fish and he is fed every day.' Self-help has also been a valued tradition in western history, from the charitable and co-operative societies to groups such as Alcoholics Anonymous, Credit Unions (which have been a notable feature of many Catholic parishes), and neighbourhood support schemes.

In the sixties community development principles became increasingly part of public policy. The Skeffington Report commended models of grassroots consultation in local planning. Local authorities built community centres and employed community workers and set up development projects in areas later to be recognized as 'urban priority areas'. Voluntary schemes also multiplied, often sponsored by the churches in collaboration with the local authority. Indeed the Government turned to community development as part of its strategy of facing industrial decline and the need for rejuvenation of the old industrial areas. A number of pilot schemes were set up by the 1964–70 Labour Government.

Community development became somewhat marginalized in the eighties and nineties, but there is presently a recovery of interest associated with the concern to develop 'social capital'.

Again it is possible to see a pattern that informs the various expressions of community development.

1 It is based on the articulation of and around the need of the community as it works on this for itself. Therefore it is about people discovering their communal identity and being enabled to take responsibility for their own future.
2 There is a belief that, in an important way, human nature is best fulfilled in relationships. This is coupled with the assertion of the worth and dignity of each individual and respect for his or her story and place in the community and the importance of releasing as far as possible their full potential.
3 There is a belief that there are resources in the local community, however deprived that community might be, which, often hidden and untapped, can be brought out and harnessed. These would include practical skills, leadership qualities and social skills.
4 Community development is both about task and about process. What is meant here is that a particular effort or project may be triggered off by a crisis or long-felt need. This provides the ostensible aim. But at the same time the members of the

community, in working towards that objective, are in the process of creating community and developing their own skills and talents. The doing of the work itself is a community-building activity and opportunity for personal development. How the project is organized and run is as important as the completion of the task. Of course it is necessary to see achievement, at least some of the time, otherwise there is loss of confidence and hope; nevertheless the gains won through doing the job may in fact be greater than the measurable results.

5 Leadership, authority and power are local, giving a sense of autonomy and ownership. Even though there will always be responsibility to others, not least councils and other providers, it is vital that those in the local context feel that they are able effectively to influence their own future.

6 Where outside resources are available, whether of leadership, as in the person of the community worker, or of specific skills, they are there for the sake of and, if at all possible, at the behest of the locals. One of the core skills of community development leadership is to seek to transfer authority to the local community. The expert should be seen as part of the team, a resource for the common endeavour.

7 Similarly, resources such as funding are to be at the disposal of the local group and under the management of the project or other activity to be used as seen fit. While reasonable accountability is to be expected, not least in complying with the law, the most important ingredient is to engender trust and freedom for responsibility.

Such a model, with its positive view of human nature and community, presupposes that all are amenable to reason and will seek the common good. It is very democratic and rests on the assumption that there is always ground for shared action and, where there is conflict, the possibility of accommodation. This does not deny that there can be bruising encounters or rough patches; but the aim is (potentially) harmony.

Nor is it easy to cope with indifference and apathy. Since, under this mode of working, community is thought of as a positive value, then lack of communal identity, whether in the individualism of the leafy suburb or in the fragmentation of the inner-city slum, is regarded as a severe lack. But it is easy then to try to impose an ideal which may be resisted or indeed be inappropriate. It is also possible to slip into a nostalgic search for the ideal community. Indeed, one of the present cries of distress in some quarters is the lack of commitment that makes it more and more difficult to recruit and retain volunteer leaders. It may well be, however, that patterns of leisure and notions of belonging are changing so that local community becomes much less cohesive than previously found in more stable neighbourhoods. As we saw in Chapter 1, there are many patterns of community and it may well be that those thought of as deprived are in fact finding their community elsewhere. Even so, it is clear that there are very many whose experience of life and community can only be described as diminished and even oppressive.

A third problem also faces community development. Communal identity is often most clearly created by contrast. This is especially true where there is a perceived enemy. 'They' want to take away 'our' shop or village school or drive a road through 'our' estate. Nimby-ism (not-in-my-back-yard) has become a feature of contemporary planning processes, whether it be an airport runway or a hostel for psychiatric patients or a travellers' camp. But what is one community's potential nemesis may be another's way to survival or a region's economic development. One of the reasons for the comparative marginalization of community work in the eighties (apart from Mrs Thatcher's dislike of independent groups) was that there were, not infrequently, cases when a community development project, including the community worker appointed by the council, found itself at loggerheads with the local authority over some planning or welfare issue. It appeared as though the very people to whom generous support had been given were turning against the 'hand that fed' them; while those 'up in arms' felt that their special and reasonable demands had not been understood or listened to. So community development can also be divisive.

A fourth issue is that community development works best in comparatively compact settings. This is not surprising since one of the points about community is the quality of human contact. This need not be at an intensive level, but there is an expectation that it will be possible to relate to the group and people within it in a reasonably immediate way. It works best in fairly small communities, the rural village or a housing estate. In the larger urban setting, community work will be through projects and centres, which may be vital for those that take part, providing them with a community base, but this can only touch relatively few of those who live and work around and be a comparatively small, though crucial, contribution to the wider context.

Nevertheless community development represents, alongside counselling and adult education, part of that humanistic flowering that was characteristic of post-war society. They share many common sources of inspiration such as Paulo Freire and Carl Rogers where the stress is laid on the process of self-development. It has certainly influenced an important strand in the life and witness of the churches, within the broad tradition of social concern, as exemplified by writers such as Fred Milsom and George Lovell.

Community action

This third strand in the skein of community work can be illustrated by reference to the fate of the community development projects set up by the Government in the sixties. The reports were almost unanimous in saying that the difficulties of the local communities were only amenable to minor amelioration so long as the wider socio-economic system was in place. The way forward is to challenge the system itself. This radicalization of community work was, of course, in line with the radicalization of politics, national and international, at the time. It appeals conceptually to an essentially Hobbesian and Marxist conflictual notion of society.

Community work under this perspective is thus closely linked to political action, such as the left-wing urban radicalism that was found in the seventies and eighties in cities like Liverpool, Sheffield and London. But even where not ideologically motivated it is clear that there are situations and issues that are not amenable to working compromises. Embedded powerful interests can withstand challenges and perhaps use their power to suppress opposition. So the only recourse is to 'up the ante' and to move into protest, demonstration and lobbying. So the first stage is the process of 'conscientization', of drawing out the areas of conflict, analysing the issues, and planning tactics and strategies. This would be true for a comparatively ordinary issue such as a school closure or opposing a bypass as much as for larger concerns such as racial justice, nuclear weapons or making poverty history.

It would seem then that a line has been crossed, albeit one that is not always clear. Yet it is important to recognize that with this move community work has moved into another mode.

1. Being confrontational there is, in some sense, an 'enemy', whether the politicians, the council or vested interests, that needs to be brought to book in some way.
2. The aim is success; the process is secondary.
3. There is an issue of legitimacy. The aggrieved party is making a claim that is not always, perhaps seldom, admitted by the other party. So there may be, for example, a challenge against the authority exercised by a political, statutory or professional body, questioning their competence and suggesting that they have not only lost the trust of the wider population but even their right to exercise power. By the same token, the challengers have to set out their right to oppose in this way, both by the logic and justice of their cause and by claiming legitimizing support.
4. The sense of being the underdog is experienced as being excluded and outside the 'corridor of power'. This can produce a frustration that exacerbates the situation and pushes those affected into taking the protests to a further level. Thus angry meetings can lead to demonstrations and frustrated demonstrations to scuffles and violence. At the extreme, violence can become the chosen means of protest, from damage to property to terrorism. Here is a set of issues that those turning to even incipient community action must be aware of and, if necessary, come to some decisions as to the limitation of their chosen means.

It is worth noting here one particular approach to community action which has a built-in philosophy of confrontation and which has been taken up in Britain, albeit in a limited way. Community Organizing is based on the work of Saul Alinski in Chicago. Its particular form reflects the social conditions in North America of radical alienation of ethnic groups and the urban poor, often highly ghettoized, and cut off from mainstream society on the one hand; and the close connections between the political and the civil authorities and big business. The only way, it is argued, that the poor can obtain their rights and secure adequate resources is to challenge the power of the elite. The strategy is to form close-knit alliances between the community leaders in an area and, through them, their constituencies. This will inevitably include the various churches and Christian missions, often ethnically based. From the strength gained through such solidarity, plans are laid to attack a series of measurable targets such as educational provision, slum landlords or sewage, and to take them on one by one. Tactics are carefully worked out and participants carefully trained (as was true for the freedom fighters in the desegregation of the South in the USA). All contact with the enemy is otherwise forbidden. There is a combination of direct confrontation in demonstration and public meeting, negotiation, electoral challenge and litigation.

These three approaches to community work, summarized in Figure 3.1 (overleaf), however, do not sit simply in contrast to each other. In practice they overlap and intertwine. There can often be a progression from one to the other. Many churches begin with a service model. They discover, for instance, that there are many lonely elderly people with no transport. So they set up a lunch club, transporting people to the church halls. This provides an important service. But this should not stop there. It does not really meet deeper needs. 'Developing' those who come is also important. This could be done by asking some users to join the steering group or asking for suggestions for further activities. Out of this could come some educational activities, an art class or an indoor gardening club. It has now moved into community development. At another point, perhaps in response to a talk, the members might write in support of a campaign for free

	Community service (responding to need)	Community development (building a community)	Community action
Typical activities	Visiting care schemes	Community centres, credit unions, self-help groups, umbrella groups, partnerships, projects	Community work and action, campaigning, lobbying
Main objectives	Support and care of individuals	Development of services, networks and coalitions at local and wider level	Community social change
Political dimension/ assumption underlying	Does not necessarily imply any change in social order, conservative	Liberal/reformist implies a fairer distribution of resources within the existing social order	Concerned to radically modify or change balance of power and resources
Attitude to change	Responding to effects of change	Accompanying change	Promoting change
Authority	Hierarchical, helper–client, donor–beneficiary	Enabling delegated	Collective
Use of power	Using power for others	Sharing power with others	Using power for/with others to effect a redistribution of power
Jesus model	Gentle Jesus healer, priest king	Leader, servant	Prophet, liberator
Theological references	Good Samaritan Jesus, friend of sinners NT models of healing	Servant Church mission Church social responsibility social gospel	Preferential option for the poor God who suffers Kingdom prophetic models, justice God/Church

Figure 3.1 Models of Christian involvement in community and neighbourhood

Source: Churches Community Work Alliance Briefing, August 1998 in *Assets for Life*. United Reformed Church 2004.

bus passes or a dial-a-ride scheme. That is community action. Groups will move in and out of the various models according to how the situation develops and the challenges that have to be met.

Modes of community work

Community-related activities come in all shapes and sizes. So there is a second set of issues to be faced alongside the question of the principles that should inform any community work. What kind of instruments should we seek to create? The answer to that is not just about the type of work envisaged but also about how the congregation sees itself in relationship to its neighbourhood and its local community. There would seem to be three main modes or types of approach, which are again not mutually exclusive but which can sit happily side by side fitting into the different aspects of a project, though it is usual for one or the other to be given priority.

The project

The key distinguishing mark of the project is that it tends to be a self-contained activity or set of activities, more or less independent from its parent body. This is indeed the most normal format for church-related community activities.

It may be very small and low key. A few members of the fellowship can get together and set up a regular group around a chosen need, opportunity or client group. Many churches have play groups or provide drop-in centres for the elderly or food for the homeless. The classic examples must be the youth club and the Women's Guild. Such projects may have been initiated through a decision of the church meeting but they run themselves and will have their own financial and management arrangements.

Other projects, however, may involve much greater professionalism, employing one or more full-time staff, raising considerable sums of money and involving detailed management and financial structures. Some will seek their own charitable status or become non-profit-making companies. It may entail a partnership with another body, such as an established children's society, to ensure that professional obligations are met and to share some of the management responsibility. In recent years there have grown up a number of organizations specifically to promote such community activities, such as Church Action with the Unemployed, Community Action Network, Employment Forum (UK) or the Church Urban Fund. Such a project can develop a range of related activities. Any such major project, however, tends to underline a perennial problem in a major way.

This is the relation of projects to the congregation. The church has been pleased to see the initiatives take off, but they take on a life of their own. This threatens a separation between the church as a worshipping body and the community activities that are associated with it. What can emerge is a church primarily there for religious activities, worship, prayer and Bible study, while community concern is for those who have a special interest. In any body of people there will indeed be those with different needs, interests, expertise and concerns, and it is good that they should find expression for their concerns within the pluriform structures of the church. But as soon as there is a move from a single-cell style of working there will be tensions. It is very difficult to hold all these activities together. Project groups with a dynamic of their own may move away from their point of origin, making the church connection purely nominal. It is certainly not unknown for a large project to dwarf the host community to the latter's disadvantage. How are diversity and a plurality of activities able to express their essential unity and coherence? This is a tricky management problem.

The community centre

A community centre is a place where a whole range of community organizations can find space and facilities. Many churches, too, often in small ways, act as community centres. Indeed, especially in some urban priority and some rural areas, the churches have the only public resources in schoolrooms and halls – itself a valuable public service. Thus, the same suite of rooms, meeting place for the weekly Bible study group and the women's meeting, youth groups and choir practice associated with the church, will also be the home for those activities that the church has sponsored, together with those outside groups who use the premises on a regular or occasional basis.

For most churches this will almost happen unconsciously and haphazardly. Others will have a policy of enabling their premises to be widely accessible. Some, however, have made the community centre their project. The buildings have been adapted or redesigned. This can include, for instance, using the former, now too large, sanctuary as hall space, sometimes by inserting a floor, exploiting former 'dead' space such as basements for games rooms, or providing specialized space for counselling or educational activities. Some have full-time community workers to manage the buildings and develop the activities.

The aim of the community centre is to provide a place of hospitality in the community, a resource that is available to all. Traditionally and to some extent this is still true in the countryside, the church stood at the centre of the village or town, a sign of God's presence and concern for the whole community. Today, the church may have been moved off centre, but it can still offer a welcome to the neighbour and stranger. The dynamic is centripetal, drawing people in. Organizations naturally find it easier to have a regular and identifiable location. There is, however, an issue of ownership. For those who use the building there has to be a sense of belonging and caring for it. This is difficult if it is always someone else's home and they are always the guests. Of course the church may well own the property, but the others need to feel part of the enterprise. In other words the centre has itself to become something of a community. This is part of the management skills required. It may mean that the congregation will find itself as one of the organizations using the facility, working alongside the other groups.

Community associations and networks

Many areas, from villages to new housing areas, have community associations. The aim is to provide some sort of umbrella organization under which the different groups and interests in the community can be linked together, often providing a forum for discussing local issues and monitoring change in the neighbourhood. It can also be the agency through which collective action can be taken. The community association frequently manages the village hall. There can also be a local news-sheet and annual events are often organized through the association. Sometimes, however, the functions that would have been undertaken by such an association are picked up, informally, by a group that somehow in practice focuses most local interests. This can range from the lounge bar in the local to the school or the cricket club and may well be the parish church or the local chapel.

The local church as part of an associational pattern of working is most likely to find its place in the community expressed in three ways. This can be seen most clearly, perhaps, at the village fête or an inner-city street carnival. First, the church members will be part of the community and contributing through the organizations of which they are members – the WI, Young Farmers, the PTA or jazz band. At the same time, and second, the church, as part of the community, uses its resources for the occasion. Its buildings can house, and the women's meeting manage the catering, or provide space for the art exhibition. Third, the church makes its own particular contribution, perhaps through a 'fair trade' stall, a special service or a float in the procession.

All this can be seen as networking. The church, its leadership and members, are involved in different aspects of local life. They are part of the natural grapevines that permeate any neighbourhood. This is formalized through structures such as community associations and carnival committees. Networking is, however, also good community pastoral practice. Clergy and other leaders know and are known by other community leaders, such as the local counsellors or community policeman or recognized key figures, from the postmistress to the retired teacher. This takes time and persistence. Through cumulative contacts there is built up a mutual trust and confidence that opens doors and brings the church closer to the mainstream of community life. This is easier in small communities. In the anonymity of the urban context it perhaps has to be more carefully planned. But there are many places where contacts can be made. It is possible to discover allies and sources of help. On the whole the church is very welcome if it brings co-operation and support. Again, in many places, those in the caring professions and community welfare meet on a regular formal basis to share concerns and, even, to discuss cases. There is an obvious advantage for the local ministers to be fully involved. The secret of all this is for others to recognize that the Christian community is a responsible partner in working for the welfare of all.

Some theological principles

A particular Christian community also needs to explore the relation between its own self-understanding and the perspectives involved in community work. In what sense does a commitment to faith shape and influence the approach to working in the wider neighbourhood? Are there any theological principles that should inform a Christian approach to community work?

When churches discuss their responsibility to the wider community one of the phrases that is bound to be used is service 'in' or 'to' the community. This would immediately suggest that the church is committed to a community service model. This is reinforced by the fact that the service model is the one most easily developed and, therefore, most frequently taken up. It also echoes significant theological language. Christ is talked of as 'the suffering servant' (Isaiah 53, echoed in Mark 10.45 and Acts 8.32–35 and elsewhere). It reflects the imperative, given to the scribe (Luke 10.25–37). Similarly, in the parable of the sheep and goats, the king rests his judgement on how compassion has been shown to the hungry, the imprisoned and the suffering (Matthew 25.31–46). That passage itself reflects Jesus' own manifesto of what it means to find the Kingdom present (Luke 4.16–21) in and through good news for the prisoner, the blind and the oppressed. Jesus' life itself was a sign of the Kingdom of God, witnessed by his treatment of the sick, the outcast, the oppressed and the lost (e.g. Mark 6.34). This is continued in the ministry of the disciples as they are sent into the villages round about (Mark 6.7–31 and parallels). Quite properly, therefore, Christians see compassion as a core faith-virtue which should be expressed both personally and through the corporate witness of the Church. And such compassion is more than the relief of individual suffering but encompasses the whole of those networks and structures that comprise human existence. It thus addresses the nature and quality of communal life in every aspect.

It cannot, however, be left to a simple appeal for Christian generosity. The notion of Christian service and the motivation behind it are more subtle and complex. Without a deeper understanding it could degenerate into 'do-goodery', seeing the other as an object of compassion and feeding a sense of well-doing and even smugness. So it is necessary to unpack the gospel and its imperatives further.

First it is important to ask: Who is being served? It is clearly, in the first instance, those who call out our compassion. Jesus, at every turn, sought the well-being of those he met and the community of which he was a part. He called himself their servant and washed their feet (John 13.12–16). So too with those who, in the name of Christ, have served those to whom they have been sent. Many, down the generations, have given of their substance and energy and authority and even their lives for the sake of others; recall Damien and the lepers, Shaftesbury and the urban poor or Martin Luther King battling against segregation. Most congregations have their memories of the unsung heroes of the faith.

Nor is it wrong for those with power, prestige, possessions and skills to use them in the service of the deprived and oppressed. The biblical notion of authority is that power is there for the good of the whole. The king, in the Old Testament (Hebrew Scriptures), is guardian of the people and the source of justice and peace. The prophets continually demanded the proper use of wealth and influence, not least in relation to the needs of the poor (e.g. Ezekiel 34; Amos 5.10–24; Micah 6.8). But this is not condescension; it is responsibility, an essential call on resources alongside meeting personal and family needs. Indeed the expectation that the impoverished and weak are to be included in the commonwealth is embedded in the Law (Torah). Tithes are for both the religious needs of the community and to support the stranger, the orphan and the widow (e.g. Leviticus 17. 8, 12; 19.10).

The notion of the stranger leads to another theme. Israel cares for the sojourner because they themselves were exiles. It is the very basis of the Torah, at the core of the Ten Commandments (Exodus 20.2; Deuteronomy 5.6). This must never be forgotten, for we share a common humanity and need compassion, support and good will. Charity is not from the strong to the weak but an expression of that necessary interdependence that makes us human. It may even be that the strong and powerful are in the greater need; they are certainly exposed to the greater judgement. Perhaps this is behind the tradition that Christ is served in the poor and the stranger. It is hinted at in Matthew 25. It is found in Russian Orthodox and Celtic spirituality. The servant is responsible to the master; but here the master is the one served as orphan and stranger.

So the question; 'Who is being served?' takes on another aspect. God in Christ is present in both those serving and those being served. Christian service is both offering Christ to the neighbour and finding Christ there in the place to which we are sent. He is there serving both the needy and ourselves as we live out the common life. Is this not part of the incarnation? Christ is part of creation, mysteriously involved in the cycle of humanity's giving and receiving.

So in the end the answer to the question is that it is God who is being served. Jesus himself was the servant of the Kingdom (Mark 1.14). He came not to do his own will but the will of the one who sent him (John 17.4–5; 5.30). So, too, the disciple is not there to conform to the patterns and demands of the world but to point to alternative possibilities (John 17.15–19). God's love for the world is that the world might be saved, might learn its true values and seek its real fulfilment (John 3.16ff.).

The act of compassionate service is thus a statement about the failure and ambiguity of the human condition. Things should not be like this and it is possible to change things for the better. It may be that it is possible only to make a small difference, a start on the road; but that is part of a wider struggle, pointing to a fuller existence. This is true whether it is expressed in supporting a single parent or comforting the dying, or in the rallying cry of 'make poverty history' or urban regeneration. In other words, there is a vision and there is a way.

This means that there has always to be an awareness of this higher authority. There can be clashes between what the community expects and what the servants of God see as the truth of the gospel. Such issues can create tensions and anxiety, even bitter divisions. For many Christians, for example, there are ethical and humanitarian issues around birth and death and gender. But faithfulness should not lead to arrogance, nor principles create aggressive certainty; for the Christian community is the servant of the servant Christ who always acts in love. He never let go of his commitment to the good of the other. Love does not give up, nor demand submission. It holds on to the tension and lives with it creatively. The 'enemy' is not there to be destroyed but loved in hope (Matthew 5.44). Nor are we exempt from the partiality and messiness of life. What we take as certainties may be prejudices or partial. To claim absolute judgement is to usurp God's place. As part of fallen humanity we constantly need the continuing mercy and saving presence of God. We also are on a pilgrimage that can lead us into unexpected places and so enlarge the truth found in Christ. For servants of the Kingdom there is always expectancy.

Crucially, too, the vision of the Kingdom is not alien or strange. The values of the Kingdom may clash with the values of the world as it is, especially in terms of the nature and exercise of power (Mark 10.42–45). Kingdom values may be derided or set aside. The claim is, however, that the Christian vision and hope corresponds to the true nature of creation and reflects the deepest longings and desires of people; that it goes along the very grain of the universe that God has implanted within it. This inner reality breaks out constantly. For instance, the desire for peace and justice, which is biblically expressed as *shalom*, is recurrent, manifested in, for example, the constant hope for peace at Christmas, in the yearnings of a parent for the welfare of a child or the idealism of a teenager. So, not surprisingly, there is a broad consensus as to what people need and what is good community: children and old people need protection, poverty is degrading and damaging, health matters and the sick are cared for, discrimination, disadvantage should be overcome and peace and justice sought. The Christian community, therefore, can work with and alongside allies and contribute to the commonwealth. As Jeremiah urged the exiles in Babylon, that is the place where you are set so 'seek the welfare of the city' (Jeremiah 29.7). Your God is not absent or powerless but to be found 'doing a new thing' (Isaiah 42.9; 43.19).

Part II

WORKING WITH ORGANIZATIONS AND PEOPLE

4

Turning towards the community

This chapter looks at an example of a congregation seeking to expand and deepen its mission in relation to the wider locality. Here we explore some of the processes involved.

Immersion in the neighbourhood

Sonia came to work in the inner city of a large city in Yorkshire which she did not know. So the first thing that she needed to do was to find out more about the area. What she did was to walk round observing carefully the buildings, the people and the neighbourhood generally. She tried to use all of her senses: sight, hearing, smell, touch. She sat in local cafés and observed the people. She noticed that the main road leading out from the city centre was busy, with small shops, built about one hundred years ago. There were Indian restaurants, sari shops, grocers selling exotic vegetables, spices and fudgy sweets, butchers selling halal meat. The people were mainly of Asian origin, but there were also whites and Africans. It was a real multiracial area, but people seemed to get on well with each other. The streets which led off were much quieter. There were large Victorian and Edwardian houses that had been mostly split up into flats, and terraces of small houses fronting directly onto the street, some with gated back alleyways. There were few cars. It seemed there had been some large industry, now closed. Sonia suspected that people in this area had little money. In one of the cafés, she met a local resident who told her that the local council was in the process of regenerating the area. He had been moved to another house in the neighbourhood, but many of his neighbours had been sent to houses in council housing estates on the outskirts of the city. The close community that had existed beforehand had been split up. Sonia looked for signs of sadness and hope. She looked to see what the area told her about the past and the future.

Later, Sonia also visited various community organizations, including two schools, a local Connexions office supporting young people, a health centre and the hospital. A local church housed a mental health project on its premises. She dropped in on various recreational facilities, all the local churches in the area, a local mosque and a gurdwara.

Sonia then decided to check out her initial impressions by looking at the local history in the city library. Her area had grown rapidly in the nineteenth century when metal working was being developed. It was not until the 1970s that people from other parts of the world, particularly the Indian sub-continent, began to buy up shops and houses in the area, congregating together, near friends and family.

Sonia also looked up the census information, from the library, and the statistics and neighbourhood pages of the internet, to obtain information about the population of the area, its ethnic make-up, and socio-economic factors such as employment, unemployment, death rates, teenage pregnancies, including the index of multiple deprivation. She then began to reflect theologically on her experiences of the area using a Bible study with members of her church and the group began to think of ways in which they might act on what they had seen.

The pastoral cycle

The process that Sonia followed to explore her area is an example of a theological reflection process known as the pastoral cycle. This (see Figure 4.1) is one of a number of tools available to enable a systematic reflection on a situation and to facilitate considered action towards given aims and objectives. It has been widely used in practical theology, having been borrowed from liberation theology and the practice of the base local communities in Latin America. Its strength is that it attempts to embody the action/reflection, praxis methodology of practical theology. Like any such tool it is simply a device for recognizing and giving structure to a process that is standard practice, especially with

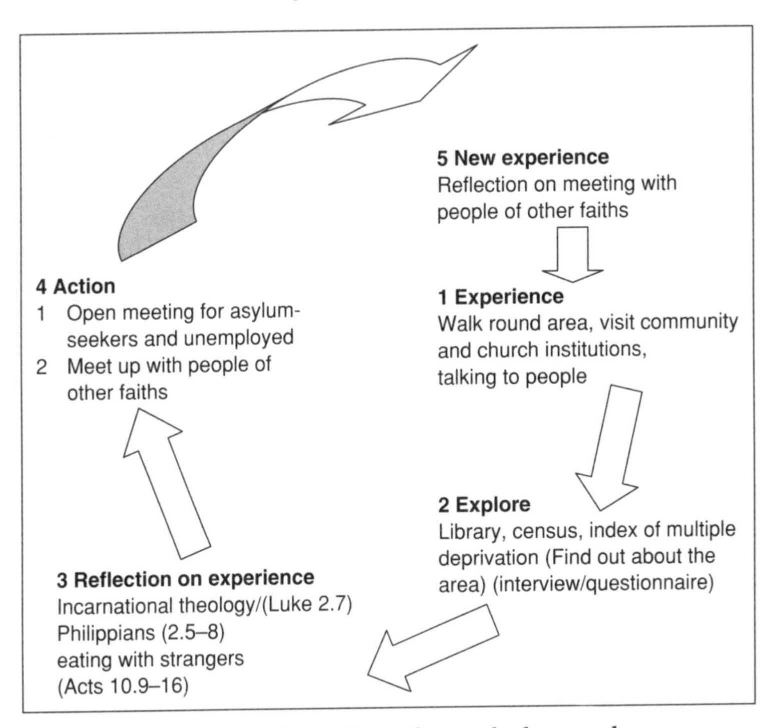

Figure 4.1 Pastoral cycle: outline of a worked example
L. Husselbee

a group or in an organization. It makes the stages of planning and action explicit. It is therefore not to be seen as a set process to be slavishly followed, for each situation will impose its own priorities and offer its own opportunities, but a checklist and reminder that certain stages and factors have to be taken into account and not bypassed when contemplating setting up community projects.

The starting point (stage 1) is *initial experience.* Something causes us to look at our situation afresh and to re-evaluate our commitments and tasks. In this case it was Sonia's arrival at her new post and the desire to learn about the situation and to explore this with her congregation. Making a community profile or audit (Figure 4.2, overleaf) is a good way to observe what is present. The initial process of exploring the area is shown as *1: Experience* on the diagram in Figure. 4.1. This is then followed by a more

To obtain an 'in-depth' description of the neighbourhood engage in the following tasks:	
1 Observation	Walk round the area, using all your senses. Talk to a random selection of people from different settings. Record: camera, tape recorder, note pad.
2 The geography	(i) Ascertain the boundaries that give shape to the location. (ii) Discover the administrative and other boundaries. (iii) Plot on a map the 'land use' and facilities in the area. • housing, different types • industries and businesses • retail • leisure and cultural facilities • health facilities • education: schools, colleges, etc. • public transport • faith organizations: churches, mosques, synagogues etc. • council provision: libraries, social services, CAB etc. • post offices and post boxes • refuse and similar facilities Record: camera, note pad, large scale map.
3 Statistics	(i) Population make up: households, gender, age, ethnicity, faith. (ii) Socio-economic data: employment, income, etc. (iii) Housing stock. (iv) Index of multiple deprivation. Resources: central library; city hall; internet. Record: maps, bar/pie charts, tables, description.
4 History	Local history, including key events, population mobility, socio-economic growth/decline, building spread. Resources: central library, museums, historical societies, newspapers, internet.
5 Human impressions	Questions: What is good/bad about living here? What do you feel about the neighbourhood? How would you improve it? What community facility is needed? Do you travel to work/shopping/leisure/family? Methods: Choose representative samples. Representative people: teachers/nurses/social workers/etc. Approach people in the street/at home/cafés/pubs/etc. Use questionnaires/formal or informal interviews. Form focus groups. Record: Filled in forms, notes, tapes, etc. Analyse both as statistics and as impressions.
6 Presenting the profile	Present material in best communicable form: e.g. formal report, public presentation, seminars etc. Ask: What are the strengths/weaknesses/opportunities/threats? Do any possibilities for action begin to appear?

Figure 4.2 Making a community profile

rigorous and analytic exploration (*2: Explore* on the diagram). She visited the local studies department in the library, researched the census statistics there and on the internet, discovering the locality's index of multiple deprivation, and interviewed a number of people. The next stage in the cycle (*3: Reflection on experience*) led Sonia and her friends to look at further Bible passages that might give them some insights into their perception of the area. They decided that asylum-seekers needed their help. Thus they arrived at *4: Action*. In this case the action followed was to set up a meeting of asylum-seekers and the unemployed and to meet up with people of other faiths, since most of the asylum-seekers came from other faith-cultures. After some time, the group arrived at *5: New experience*, and the whole process began again, assessing where they had got to and what the next steps were. We look at these stages in further detail in the following pages.

Making a community profile

We have followed Sonia as she began her voyage of discovery in a new neighbourhood. However, if they were to take up this challenge it must be done on the basis of a realistic evaluation, achieved from carefully researched information. The church has to discover the real needs of the community and whether it is able to respond in a creative and sustained way. A systematic approach to this is to make a community profile or to conduct a parish audit. This is the first part of stage 2 of the pastoral cycle.

Figure 4.2 outlines this process and suggests what needs to be looked for and methods and resources that are available. These are not here spelled out in detail as they are fully described in the literature, some of which is mentioned in the text and/or in the bibliography. Special reference, however, is made to making best use of the statistical information that is available, and that is often overlooked in this process.

Base maps

It is very useful to obtain as large a scale map of the local area as possible, such as an Ordnance Survey 1:2500, or 1:10,000, or the Site plan or Super plan, which will have buildings detailed, or if this is not obtainable, a good street map. Large-scale plans are not always easy to obtain, but are sometimes available at large bookshops. The Ordnance Survey gives lists of suppliers. If the local council has plans for developing the neighbourhood, sometimes the research on the area is available on large maps. Major public libraries also have local studies departments which carry historical and most current planning documents.

Population statistics

Major public libraries carry census documents. One difficulty with these statistics is that they can easily be out of date. It is now possible, however, to obtain local population statistics from the internet, although finding them for your precise ward can sometimes be difficult, but it is possible to enter a postcode in order to gain more specific information. Local councils have often analysed local population statistics and drawn maps and bar charts showing such factors as employment, single-parent families, and crime. Until 2003, the unit of measurement was the electoral ward. After 2004, however, the unit of measurement has been the Super Output Area (see census web). For statistical purposes the country has been divided into small blocks of land called Output Areas. These allow us to look in more detail at much smaller local areas. Output Areas have been combined to form two layers of Super Output Areas known as Lower Layer Super Output Areas (LSOAs) and Middle Layer Super Output Areas (MSOAs).

Index of multiple deprivation

When a number of statistics for various socio-economic factors have been brought together an index of multiple deprivation can be arrived at. In 2004, these factors were:

- employment deprivation
- income deprivation
- health deprivation
- barriers to housing and services
- education, skills and training deprivation

- living environment deprivation
- crime

These factors are averaged and ranked against all the wards, or Super Output Areas (SOAs), in the UK. In England, in 2000, there were 8,414 wards, and, in 2004, there were 32,482 Local Super Output Areas. A ward ranked as 1 is the most deprived in the country. This gives us a league table for socio-economic ratings. SOAs with a high ranking of social deprivation attract government grants, which will vary slightly according to the given scheme. This is one of the reasons for knowing the index of multiple deprivation for your area. Figure 4.3 illustrates this by setting out a comparison of urban deprivation; and Figure 4.4 (overleaf) for selected wards in Manchester. It can be seen, in the latter case, that wards to the north and east in the inner city and the large council estate to the south have the highest multiple deprivation.

Of course, knowing the index of multiple deprivation may appear to be more important when working in a deprived urban

District Name	Average of SOA ranks	Average SOA scores	Extent	Local Concentration	Income Scale	Work Scale
Top 5 most deprived districts in England (based on average of SOA ranks)						
Hackney	1	5	1	47	9	26
Tower Hamlets	2	4	2	22	8	34
Manchester	3	2	4	3	3	3
Islington	4	6	3	44	30	38
Liverpool	5	1	5	2	2	2
Other core cities						
Nottingham	9	7	9	9	10	12
Birmingham	16	15	14	15	1	1
Newcastle	48	20	24	5	19	10
Bristol	68	67	71	34	14	14
Sheffield	82	60	51	30	6	5
Leeds	91	68	64	24	4	4

Figure 4.3 District-level ranks

Source: English Indices of Deprivation 2004, ODPM June 2004. Crown copyright. Source http://www.manchester.gov.uk/planning/studies/census/pdf accessed 19.4.06.

L. Husselbee

Ward	Rank
■ Harpurhey	2
■ Miles Platting & Newton Heath	4
■ Ardwick	59
■ Hulme	81
■ Moss Side	180
■ Longsight	225
■ Rusholme (housing)	2703

Figure 4.4 Index of multiple deprivation for selected wards in Manchester, 2004

<www.manchester.gov.uk/planning/studies/census/pdf/F2_IMD_2004.pdf> accessed 19.10.05 reissued 2004 and over new wards 2004.

L. Husselbee

area, but neighbourhood statistics such as these can be also useful for those living in rural areas, which can also hide deprivation, and also for those in 'well-off' areas where deprivation can appear to be not a problem.

All this information gathered about the neighbourhood and its setting, together with the material gathered from other sources, as in Figure 4.2, can then be collated and shared with the wider congregation. This might be done in the form of a printed report, articles in the church magazine, exhibitions and presentations, conferences or seminars, or a combination of all or several of these. This is stage 1 of the exploration. Stage 2 is to seek how to respond.

The church audit

Having identified unmet needs in the community, a church can then begin to think about how they might engage with the community. As can be seen in Chapter 2, it is important at this stage that the church doesn't just think about what they can do *for* the local community (community service), but also considers how they might involve the community itself (community development) or even what kind of campaigning they might need to do to improve things (community action). If a clear need emerges, however, then it is important to consider what resources might be available to meet that need. It might be that a church can offer its premises so that the local council or another voluntary organization can provide an activity. It may be that the church might consider seeking funds to employ a person or persons to set up a project, or it may be that the church is able, with its own volunteer support, to set up its own project. So an audit of what the church is realistically able to contribute needs to be carried out. This needs to be as thorough as the community audit, looking at current activities, the membership, buildings and finance. It might be achieved through church meetings, small discussion groups and working parties and/or a questionnaire of the church members, adherents or parish roll designed to discover what volunteers might realistically wish to offer to any project. It, too, needs to be well presented so that the whole community can make informed decisions.

The congregation as community resource

One of the most significant discoveries that Sonia and her congregation made was to recognize how far they were already engaged with the community as a congregation. As soon as they had started to ask about possibilities of working in the neighbourhood, their horizons had broadened and they saw things differently. Few and elderly as the congregation was, they were, for the most part, themselves from the streets around. They were repositories of a great deal of information of a kind that was hidden in the statistics. They were guardians of the local memory. They went in and out of the local shops, got their pensions until recently from the post office, knew their neighbours and listened to the local gossip. They already had contact with the newcomers into the district, even if it were only by greeting those who lived next door. Some had, in fact, begun to get to know them better, baby-sitting on occasion or having errands run by the children living in the street. It was also true that some key members of the congregation were locally well known. Meg cleaned at the school, Sally was a lollypop lady on the school crossing, Molly was a receptionist at the health centre, Bill was one of the gardeners in the park, and James was a special constable, enjoying being on duty at the soccer games on a Saturday afternoon. A few worked in local shops and one couple ran a small newsagents. Two or three were active in local politics, of whom one was a councillor for the ward. Add all this together and it amounted to a great deal of information that could be built on. It also represented real, living connections with those around. This is the place from which the church's self-appraisal should start, a platform from which to launch any initiative.

The congregation as community

Sonia also saw that the process she had inaugurated had begun to have profound effects on the congregation itself. Three things were happening which reinforced each other. First, there was a new sense of purpose. They slowly lost their introspective anxiety and looked beyond the long-standing routines. When it became clear that, limited as they were, it was possible realistically to take up some of the challenges, then it became a buzz. There was an atmosphere of anticipation and hope, a belief that they were there for others.

Second, people began to grow in confidence and open out. They learnt new things about each other, inducing a sense of respect. Indeed there were some surprises. Dolly found she had a real aptitude for meeting people and getting them talking. James surprised himself as secretary of the audit committee. Mary enjoyed managing the premises and hiring them out. For all of them, mundane tasks which had been done for many years now became more worthwhile. Every contribution to the life of the congregation, not just those that were active in the audit, was valued. Some found it possible to take on fresh tasks.

Third, meetings were constructive, even if some of the issues were contentious. Worship had an added reality. There was a camaraderie that had previously been missing. Yet there was a new openness. Those who began to join them, some for the first time and some to return, found a welcome and a desire to incorporate them in the life of the congregation.

It was not easy, nor without hitches. Some did not want to be disturbed and others were fearful and hesitant. With patience and wise leadership, however, Sonia was able to rejoice in what was happening. All this was itself community development. The very process had been creative both for the group and for each member. Working with the congregation is a community-building activity and calls for community-work skills and approaches.

Theological reflection

The third stage of the pastoral cycle is theological reflection. Through Bible study and prayer, the congregation began to catch a gospel vision as to how their small community could relate to the changing neighbourhood. This continued throughout the process and confirmed them in their journey. What this might entail and some of the themes that would have been taken up are to be found from time to time throughout this book (see Chapters 2, 5, 10, 11).

The mechanics of setting up a project

If the needs are there and there are sufficient resources within the congregation, the church can think seriously about setting up a project or undertaking a specific activity. This is stage 4 of the pastoral cycle. But any such projects should not be undertaken lightly. The mechanics of setting up a project include issues of responsibility and ownership, management and legal requirements. Sometimes members of churches believe that since any work that they do for the community is part of God's mission, the kinds of management used in secular or paid situations is not for them. They may believe in any case that the priest or minister is 'in charge'. But churches have a responsibility to support anyone who works with them and to make sure that adequate provision is made in relation to financial and employment issues. Even within the voluntary sector, a proper management structure needs to be set up before any employment of staff or work takes place. For example, a project will need to set up some kind of governing body or management committee which should meet on a regular basis. This should represent and be responsible to the sponsors of the project such as the church or the local authority. If the project is a charity then the members of the managing committee are also trustees who must work to the rules of the Charity Commission, and are personally responsible for any financial irregularity or failure. So the church might like to consider setting up some financial protection for them. The governing body, which might be called a board of trustees, board of governors, board of directors, executive committee or steering committee, or some other term, should include representatives of the sponsoring body, paid and/or volunteer workers, and users of the project. The meeting will need to be chaired and there will need to be a proper agenda and minutes. Audited accounts will need to be presented on an annual basis to an annual general meeting. Depending on the size of the project, this could be incorporated in the church's AGM. Management committees will need initial and regular training. The Shaftesbury Society, among a number of similar bodies, provides regular training days, and books such as Sandy Adirondack's provide helpful advice.

The governing body will need, at an early point, to appoint someone to manage the project on a day-to-day (or week-to-week) basis. If the position is to be a paid one then proper attention needs to be given to equal opportunities good practice. The position, or positions, will need to be advertised and applicants interviewed, including attention given to their having suitable qualifications, and care taken that no favouritism is shown. Such a process may not appear to be appropriate when a volunteer from the church becomes the manager, especially if the work is on a very small scale, but attention to good employment practice can still usefully apply. Once the appointment has been made, it is not the managing body's role to get involved in day-to-day decisions. Their role is that of overall strategy, worked at in negotiation with and with the co-operation of the manager. Managers should be able to make their own day-to-day decisions within an agreed strategy and budget. Sometimes churches, usually those with a congregational polity where decisions are taken through the church (community) meeting, have a culture which leads some members to think that it is their task, as members, to be involved in every decision, and this attitude can lead to considerable tensions, especially with paid full-time managers. For example, a grant received just before the end of the financial year which needs to be spent quickly is much better managed by the manager, provided that the process for applying for the grant has been agreed by the management committee. Church decision-making processes can take too long. If the day-to-day manager is of the same status as the priest or minister (such as a theologically trained Church Related Community Worker), then care needs to be taken to recognize this equal status.

The legal implications of any project need to be checked out at an early stage by contacting an appropriate solicitor, a similar local church or secular project, or the local authority. Premises may need to be inspected to ensure that health and safety guidelines are kept. Whenever catering is involved there are stringent hygiene regulations which must be followed. For example, at least one responsible person needs to have undertaken and passed a hygiene course (available at a local further education college), and kitchens need to have more than one sink (one for washing hands). If regulations require the church to have better facilities it may be possible to apply for a community or local authority grant to carry out this work. Ask the local Community Chest for advice. Churches also need to consult their denominational good practice guidelines in relation to children. Much of the concern about meeting the legal and technical requirements, which can be very onerous and time-consuming, can be more easily met by working in partnership with a recognized body that will provide the professional back-up. Several of the older children's charities work in this way (see Chapter 7 for details).

In every case, whether it is a low-key piece of work using local volunteers or a more major project involving considerable sums, preparation is paramount. Are all the elements in place? These include premises, equipment, outside contacts, publicity, finance and personnel. Above all, has the Christian community begun to appreciate what it means to undertake these new tasks, to be host to those who may be strangers, sharing premises with new groups, working with others who may not share the same expectations?

Witness to the reality of Christ?

Sonia and her church firmly believed that helping to support the increasing numbers of asylum-seekers and refugees in their area was part of their mission and witness to the reality of Christ. They decided to open the doors of their church hall every Thursday afternoon and Friday mornings creating a drop-in centre that they decided to call 'The Sanctuary'. A management committee, comprising members of the church, decided to apply to the local authority for a grant so that they could employ a church-related community worker and alter the premises to provide better toilets and a new kitchen. They also invited other organizations to come in to share their expertise. Sure Start set up a crèche; representatives from the local employment office came to suggest possibilities for work; the local further education college sent tutors to teach English as a foreign language; and a church member who was a retired solicitor agreed to help with legal advice.

At first, there was no overt reference to the Christian faith. But as time went on, new members of the governing body, who were also volunteers, began to push for more public Christian witness while the asylum-seekers and refugees were present. They also discouraged offers of help from users from the Middle East. This caused tensions with some of the other volunteers, who felt that this denied respect to the Muslim faith of many of the users. The users didn't say much, but it was noticed that some were not coming any more. The manager and the governing body met to consider the situation. There was a split in opinion. The managing body prayed about the issue and they read Philippians 4.1–9, considering the argument between Euodia and Syntyche. They realized that quarrels in the church were as common in New Testament times as now. They also found that Paul suggested a kind of spiritual exercise, designed to drive out bad thoughts and create positive feelings towards others: that they should not stoke up their anxiety, but pray about things instead, letting their minds think about good, beautiful, honourable things. Having worked it through, the management committee produced a policy statement, which said that there would be no active Christian teaching at the Sanctuary, but that it would be possible to leave leaflets around describing the Christian faith, and that a brief description of the Christian faith would be pinned up on the wall together with descriptions about Islam, Hinduism and the Buddhist faiths. Information about worship would be available on the notice board. It was also agreed to invite two users on to the governing body.

Such differences in theology can produce situations which need to be handled carefully and with skill. These issues especially arise when local authorities insist that any grant that they might give is on condition that no Christian information should be imparted. It is then up to the church to decide whether or not to accept such grant offers. Certainly, project-workers need to be sensitive to the needs and beliefs of the people that they are working with.

Differences between urban priority, suburban and rural settings

Sonia's church was in an urban priority area, which made a considerable difference. Grants from the local authority were relatively easy to obtain because the high index of multiple deprivation attracted Government New Deal money. The local Sure Start government initiative, set up to support work with very young children, was looking for premises to expand its work. It was also relatively easy to find volunteers to help, because many people who came to the church and who lived in the area were long-term unemployed. The opportunity to meet with friends to support others and (as a perk) to have a free lunch, encouraged many people to help.

The situation in a 'well-heeled' suburb, where most people live in owner-occupied houses and where many work very long hours, makes setting up a project much more difficult. It is not that there is no need; people in need are often hidden in their own homes. Many, especially the elderly and bereaved, are very lonely, looking out on empty streets while their neighbours are away all day. Would-be volunteers are mostly too busy to help, though they might offer cash. It is difficult to find local authority grants.

Such churches, however, should not be discouraged from working in and with the community. It may well be possible to find retired people and those without full-time work to volunteer to work in such activities as carers' and toddlers' schemes, holiday clubs, good neighbour schemes, clubs for the elderly and stroke victims. Funding may need to be raised by church members or by charging a small fee for services. It may also be valuable to set up church-twinning schemes with church community projects in social priority areas, which can use people with skills found among professionals, such as accountancy, teaching, counselling and so forth.

Similarly, the needs and opportunities in rural areas are different. Here too, in many places deprivation is very high, although often hidden. Transport costs add to people's difficulties. Many are paid very low wages. Churches have to match, if possible, the needs of those areas. For example, support through telephone contacts. Opportunities for farmers, faced with losing markets, to meet will help to counteract the high rate of suicide among farmers. In really deprived communities, second-hand furniture, white goods, clothing and food can be sold for small sums which can help to fund workers. These areas can attract government and lottery grants more easily than areas with higher multiple indexes of deprivation. It is easier, however, to set up projects, as in urban priority areas, in rural areas where poverty has been identified by the Government. So the key is to know your local area, know your church, discover where resources lie and decide what, if anything, your church can do to support the local community, or even someone else's community.

5

Living with ethnic, cultural and religious diversity

This chapter is about how, in a pluralistic society, churches and community projects need to look at anti-oppressive practices. What are the issues relating to the prejudice that occurs between people living in different ethnic, cultural and religious communities and what measures can be undertaken to counteract these? But there are other forms of difference that raise similar questions, such as gender and disability. The causes are often related to fear of people who are different or a desire to exercise power, even if this is not consciously done. But this is not anything new. It has been part of human existence from time immemorial, though it has apparently become more acute in recent years, especially after 9/11 in New York in 2001 and 7/7 in London in 2005.

Racial diversity

When Phil first came to the city-centre church in the West Midlands twenty years ago there were about thirty grey-haired members of the congregation (mostly women). Then one day a young Ghanaian student, named Israel, came to the church. Phil was painfully aware that many people in the congregation were less than welcoming. He was also aware of the difficulty that many West Indian immigrants had had in integrating in many traditional English churches. Eventually many black Christians had left to start up their own. Phil did not want this to happen. Of course, he understood the insecurities and fears of the white congregation. But if the church was to survive, then it needed to relate to the new ethnic groups round the church, mostly much younger than the white population. What was Phil to do?

If he encouraged Israel and his friends, then some of the church members had threatened to leave. He embarked on a programme of education. He preached on welcoming the stranger, and the house groups considered how this could happen. To make Israel feel welcome they learned some Ghanaian hymns and songs. They began to take an interest in Israel's background and studies. Gradually, more Christians from many parts of the world came. Wherever possible, they used hymns and songs in the different languages, allowed everyone to say the Lord's Prayer in their own language, and occasionally asked newcomers to lead prayers in their own tongue. It took a long time to persuade the white congregation to accept newcomers in leadership positions. One or two white members left, but the church went on growing. Some of the immigrants had tried other churches, but they came back after having found that they had not been really welcomed. Recently, Phil baptized a child from an Algerian family and asked them to make their promises in Arabic.

Phil believes that eating together is an important way for all to come together and know each other. Most of these parties happen on Sundays after morning worship, when there is also an education programme in small groups. This is especially important as this is more than a local church. People come from miles around. There are a number of rooms for gathering and eating, but they also use part of the manse garden.

Egbert Rooze, a Protestant pastor working in Belgium, has a similar approach to overcome divisiveness. He calls this 'No room at the inn' theology which is centred on a ministry of hospitality based on Matthew 10.16 and Mark 7.34 ('"Ephphatha!" (which means, "Be opened!"')). Rooze finds that there are two factors which hinder the church from becoming truly missionary: first, when the church is not aware of what is really happening in its society, and second, when it does not have an Ephphatha-mind. 'Both', he says, 'go hand in hand. When you open up your mind, you also become aware of hardship in the world.' He comments: 'In Europe, and especially in Britain, we don't see representative proportions of multicultural nations in our churches. Why? Many immigrants are Christians from

Africa, Asia, and the Middle East. They tend to worship separately in their own national groups. This is a pity because we could enrich one another.' Rooze has found that those coming from abroad don't mind about their own identity. They are looking, in the first instance, for a living, human, biblical, warm church which is caring for their needs. Rooze has also discovered that an '*ubuntu*-community' is important; this means to become more and more an eating and drinking community. He also believes that a church should use as many opportunities as possible to celebrate.

When Phil's church first began also to open its doors to asylum-seekers and refugees the church was swamped by the media asking why the church was welcoming such people. The British National Party, which had a strong following in the area, accused the church of breaking the law because they were sheltering illegal immigrants. This was a very difficult time, especially as other local churches took fright and would not have anything to do with asylum-seekers. It took considerable courage to persist.

Racism

Many countries are becoming more and more multicultural. This can bring about a great richness of society as people of a variety of ethnic and cultural backgrounds live alongside one another, but it can also engender prejudice and hatred, which is usually directed at minority groups. This is racism which has been defined by Katz (in Thompson 2001, p. 65) as 'prejudice plus power'.

What can be done to combat racism? One of the most important ways is by recognizing our own racial prejudices. This can be best done by finding opportunities to get to know people from different backgrounds. It is also important to recognize positive black identities and to take seriously differences in culture, not ignoring differences by taking a 'colour-blind' attitude.

One of the first ways in which prejudice can be tackled is through education and a willingness to challenge oppressive practice. This can require considerable courage, but if no one is prepared to challenge behaviour that excludes others, then we are colluding in the prejudice. One of the key attributes for anyone wishing to work in the community is, therefore, to acquire anti-oppressive practice skills. Where there are needs they have to be recognized. Positive discrimination is sometimes controversial. To advertise posts in journals that are read by the black community is important. We also need to challenge racist attitudes, even when they are voiced by 'dear old ladies'. This can include official structures. For example, one church-related community worker went to a great deal of trouble to support a young man who had been erroneously arrested by the police, she believed, simply because he was black, involving the local Councillor and MP. Some churches and Churches Together have successfully run anti-racist courses for local institutions, including the police. But churches themselves are by no means immune. Most denominations (with the exception of black-led churches), are largely white-led. Despite some exceptions, most priests and ministers are still white, and the proportion of deacons or elders or churchwardens do not represent the ethnic mix of a congregation. Many black members are reluctant to put themselves forward. But there are, happily, some excellent examples of the church and community working hard to produce anti-racist attitudes.

Government policy has long sought to counter racism, ever since setting up the Race Relations Commission under the Race Relations Act. The New Labour Government has had social inclusion as one of its major policies, which includes working against racial discrimination. The latest initiative came on 24 August 2006, when the Government minister Ruth Kelly launched the Commission on Integration and Cohesion.

How is it possible to find ways of bringing together ethnic and cultural groups which may have very different ideas about what it means to live in a strange land, often exacerbated by economic and generational disparities? This is going to be a long and perhaps painful transition, the future and shape of which is not by any means clear. The process will include, however, hard intellectual debates as well as cultural and social upheavals. The Christian community cannot but be engaged in the process, rediscovering and reshaping itself on the way. But from a Christian point of view, while there is no obvious answer to this issue, there is a gospel imperative to treat everyone with dignity and worth, even in the face of hatred and enmity, as the neighbour that God has given us, being pastorally sensitive and seeking justice and true peace (*shalom*).

Phil and the congregation that welcomed Israel, of course, were working within the bounds of a common faith. The question for the churches is also: how does the experience of unity and diversity in Christ help us in living alongside other faiths?

Encountering other faiths

Raj comes from a village in India. He grew up in a Christian household in an area where most people practised the Hindu faith. At school, Raj was at best teased, and at worst, bullied. After working for a Christian organization as a youth leader Raj applied for missionary service to the United Kingdom. He was sent with his wife and small son to a town in the West Midlands, with a high number of people of Asian origin in the community, most of whom were practising Muslims. Here Raj found himself living in a minority faith again. He looked as if he were an Asian Muslim. He spoke their local language. Raj's task as a missionary was to work for his local group of Christian churches, to make contact with people, particularly those of other faiths, and to enable people from the Christian churches to be in dialogue with them. At first, Raj struggled to understand the small and elderly English Christian churches, who did not really want to make contact with Asians: they were foreigners, to be treated warily. Neither group really understood the other.

Raj began slowly. It was decided to hold a sports day for Muslims and Christians. There would also be fancy dress, and food. Invitations went out. At first, people were a little wary, but they began to turn up. Parents came to support their children. People from the two groups gradually began to learn more about one another and to discover that they were, as people, not so different. They decided to hold another day for Hindus and Christians, and even began to discuss holding a multifaith worship occasion. Personal contact, they agreed, had certainly been of key importance. Meeting people from other faiths is perhaps the most helpful way of finding out about others. There are books which are useful to obtain a comprehensive background to a faith, its history, beliefs and practices. But there is, in the end, nothing like discovering what it means in people's actual lives, in their homes and as they go about their daily business.

Finding ways of communicating

Karen, who had taken part in Raj's 'other faith' days, wanted to take it further by, in a simple way, experiencing another faith from within. So she decided to wear a *hijab* (the Muslim head scarf) for a day. The women in the shop were very helpful and told her that the Koran instructs women to be modestly clothed in public. Hands, face and feet are the only parts of the body to be seen. This immediately raised the differences in Islam itself. How is this to be carried out in modern western society? It is also an issue for the authorities in a pluralist society. Schools, for instance usually allow girls to wear a *shalwar kameez* (tunic and trousers) but not a *jilbab* (loose dress). This has caused some controversy. There is also the problem of the *burka* (full veil) in certain circumstances. On the other hand there are those who feel they have met the Koranic injunction by adopting modest western dress. And some would even want to interpret the Koran from a feminist point of view, claiming equality for women in every respect (Amina Waud). More practically, Karen found that wearing the *hijab* meant that she had to relate to people in very different ways. She was the stranger, averting her eyes, relating to men differently, deferring to others and remembering what it was she was permitted to eat. It was useful not only to understand her new Muslim friends better, but also to recognize some of the negative attitudes of the British.

Biblical reflection

In relation to ethnic and religious diversity, the bottom line for the Christian faith comes at the climax of the argument in Ephesians. 'I bow my knees before the Father, from whom every family in heaven and earth takes its name' (3.14–15). God is the creator and redeemer of 'every tribe and tongue' and, therefore, in God, we are all one (Galatians 3.28; Colossians 3.11; see Romans 1—3). But in practice this has not been recognized or sustained. Indeed the Bible itself has been and is used as justification and authority for racial discrimination: the anti-Semitism of the pro-Nazi German Christians, in support of apartheid, or of a theology of the land. Perhaps, more germane to our time is the post-exilic nationalism expressed in Ezra-Nehemiah and the purity tradition that ran through Pharisaic practice and among the Essenes and Zealots in Jesus' time and beyond. This was something that the early Church had also to face before admitting the Gentiles as equals to the Jewish believers (see Galatians 3 and Acts 10—11.18). Even Jesus, for whom the children of Israel came first, seems to have had to be challenged by the Syro-Phoenician woman (Mark 7.24–30). At the same time, however, it is clear that Jesus saw the Kingdom as universal (Matthew 8.11). He not only healed the Syro-Phoenician's child but also the servant of the Roman centurion (Matthew 8.5–11) and mixed with Samaritans (John 4; see Luke 10.29–37). This comprehensive perspective, however, is deeply rooted in the whole biblical tradition. Genesis 1—11 not only tells of the effects of human sin but asserts that God is creator and Lord of all. Isaiah (40—55) affirms the omnipotence of God over history and creation and is echoed as a protest tradition in the post-exilic community in, for example, Isaiah 60, Ruth and John.

The Church, too, quickly saw its mission in inclusive terms. Acts 2 deliberately describes the Pentecostal gift in terms of being understood in every human language. It does not reverse Babel but affirms the variety within the unity. This is important as the Church has too often reversed the early insight and sought to make the unity dominate the variety, enforcing conformity. In the new Jerusalem, however, the nations are expected to bring each their own riches (Revelation 21.24). In Christ the whole creation finds its fulfilment (Colossians 1.15–23). But this threatens to introduce again a note of exclusivism, a stance that has indeed been abused by Christians, when they see Christ solely in terms of the Church, giving support to crusades and forced conversions. Perhaps, however, there are hints in the Bible of another way. First there is, as we have seen, a positive affirmation of variety and respect for other cultures and traditions. God is at work outside the bounds of faith (see Isaiah 40—45). Second, it is Jesus who is the clue we are to follow in understanding God's creative and redemptive purposes. So it is important to cling to him in faith and to grow into a fuller understanding of his grace, which is itself all-embracing (Ephesians 4.1–16). As we do this, third, we find we are more and more open to the other, living with and for them in love and peace and justice because our hearts have been garrisoned by the peace of God (Philippians 4.7). 'Perfect love casts out fear' (1 John 4.18). That love, however, is the love God has for us and all creation, which he gives us to fill our lives, a love which we give back to God and exercise in relation to our neighbour. But only gradually are we drawn into that grace, for our hearts and our churches are stubborn and culturally hidebound. This is a struggle that is never-ending (Romans 7.14–20).

Gender and sexual orientation

Prejudice in these areas is primarily found in two forms. First, there is the discrimination against women in our society. It is acknowledged that women are often socially and economically disadvantaged. Women earn less and are disproportionately underrepresented in the higher reaches of the professions, public life and commerce. They are tied more closely to the home and tend to be expected to deal with the domestic chores. Where there is poverty it is often the woman that carries the burden, not least in single-parent families. Women are seen as having the caring, nuturing role in contrast to the male aggressive stance. Although gender stereotypes are breaking down, discrimination against women is still present. This is especially so in relation to domestic violence and abuse and rape (Thompson 2001, p. 41).

The churches, too, have been part of this pattern of discrimination. Traditionally the women have taken the subordinate roles, confined to the welfare and educational ministries. The ordination of women is still contentious, even within the Free

Churches which have been comparatively liberal. The Church of England is still divided and now faces conflict over women bishops. Among Catholics and the Orthodox the issue is not absent but institutionally suppressed.

Feminism, as it has evolved from its early roots in radical Protestantism and the Enlightenment, has been marked by a number of different stances, from a radicalism that wanted women to have their own separate identity and culture to those simply seeking equal opportunities in society; from those who would stress the feminine traits that mark a woman in contrast to a man to those that see women and men as essentially the same; from those who would argue that all women are fighting a common cause to those who recognize that women have different issues in different cultural settings.

A second, somewhat different and yet interwoven set of issues are posed by the lesbian and gay community and others such as bisexuals and transsexuals. Here the distinguishing issue is of sexual practice. This rouses considerable feelings in sections of the 'straight' community, often moving beyond the rational. From the point of view of this discussion the central issue is that of discrimination and their place in the Church and the wider community. Increasingly they have won recognition and acceptance. This has recently been acknowledged in the UK by the introduction of Civil Partnerships, affording the gay community legal rights similar to those afforded to married couples. Also lesbian and gay persons have more and more been able to exercise parental rights or adopt children.

Within the churches the acceptance or rejection of lesbian and gay persons has engendered heated theological debate, especially over ordination. This has resulted in an institutional conservatism, wary of change and schism. As a result, lesbian and gay persons and others have increasingly been marginalized and have had to resort either to continuing to suppressing their identity or to seeking fellowship in those congregations where they are welcomed and/or in separate groupings such as the Lesbian and Gay Christian Movement.

Feminist theology has had almost as wide a range of perspectives as the wider movement. It would not be unfair, however, to see its main thrust as a kind of more or less radical revisionism. While some would reject the tradition as irredeemably patriarchal and declare themselves as post-Christian, most would want to reclaim the tradition by unearthing other suppressed traditions which are claimed to be inherent in the faith and, on that basis, to represent Christian understanding. Not least has this been done in relation to the biblical material, where there are some surprising and stunning examples (given the culture of the time) of the way in which women have much to contribute and play significant roles. Not least is this true of Jesus' story. At his birth are Elizabeth and Mary (Luke 1.24–45), and the women, including Mary Magdalene, are the first to witness his resurrection (John 20.1–18). Jesus also includes women in his ministry: the unclean woman suffering from haemorrhages (Matthew 9.18–22, Luke 8.43–48), the woman caught in adultery (John 8.1–11), Mary and Martha (John 11.1–44) and Luke tells us that there were women in the band of disciples (23.49). In the early Church, too, women played key roles, including leadership. 'There is no longer Jew or Greek, there is no longer slave or free, there is no longer male and female; for all of you are one in Christ Jesus' (Galatians 3.28); 1 Corinthians 7 ensured that Christian widows and others were provided with a family in the Church rather than be alone in a hostile society; Lydia (Acts 16.11–15) and Phoebe and others in Romans 16 were elders or missionaries. For some commentators it is also important that Wisdom, in both Hebrew (*chokmah*) and Greek (*sophia*) is a feminine noun, suggesting that there is a feminine dimension in the Godhead itself.

The issues of homosexuality have not, until recently, been widely discussed. The controversy relates to two primary issues. The first pertains to an understanding of natural law, whether sexual activity is to be limited to heterosexual activities within marriage; and even here there is no consensus. The other is about the use and status of the Bible as a rule book. Despite crucial ambiguities about the use of the Torah in the Christian tradition, it is assumed that in this case it can be read off straight, especially as kinds of homosexual activity appear in some Pauline lists of sinful behaviour (but then so does gossiping!).

It is impossible here to resolve such complex and deep-seated arguments. Perhaps, however, the following can be said. Jesus (Mark 12.28–34) Paul (Romans 13.12) and John (John 13.34) all declare that the basis of human relationships, and hence of the Law, is love. If so, the issue is less about specific acts of behaviour and more about inward attitudes. Perhaps the first question to be asked of any relationship is whether it expresses genuine love. Is it not possible to see love expressed in a whole range of relationships? Is anyone excluded? What is Jesus saying to those who would sit in judgement? Whose party would Jesus go to (Matthew 9.11)? We start, therefore, with our common humanity.

Prejudice due to lack of physical or mental ability

A new word has been coined to describe the systematic discrimination and prejudice that occurs against people who have any kind of physical or mental disability and which oppresses and degrades them: 'Disablism refers to the combination of social forces, cultural values and personal prejudices which marginalises disabled people, portrays them in a negative light, and thus oppresses them' (Thompson 2001, p. 112). Disablism, for example, assumes that physically disabled people are ill, or lack intelligence, and therefore includes the tendency to treat them like children or be patronizing towards them. These kinds of attitudes were well illustrated by the title of the radio programme for the disabled, *Does He Take Sugar?* Disabled people can be the object of revulsion and negative attitudes. Jokes are told at the expense of the disabled. Many, in the past, were hidden away in institutions, and some disabled people today fear going into public places. At the other extreme, disabled people can be overprotected and 'done good to'. But often their needs are just ignored because decisions are made with the 'standard' person in mind. For example, although spaces are provided on some trains and buses for wheelchairs, it may be difficult to get on to the vehicle in the first place, or seats designed for standard people may not be suitable for those who are vertically challenged or extra tall. Despite the 2004 Disability Act of Parliament in the UK, many buildings (including many places of worship) do not have easy access for disabled people such as ramps or Braille notices. It is of no help to say, 'We have no disabled people here so we don't need to bother providing such access', if disabled people cannot access a building in the first place. There is also a strong relationship between disability and poverty. There is a tendency to treat disabled people as problems, rather than as people with problems caused by the social arrangements which undermine their autonomy and exclude them from mainstream society. Some people also suffer a kind of 'double jeopardy'. For example, those who are both aged and disabled or women and disabled may be especially ignored, unless they are a sporting celebrity such as Tanni Grey Thompson. Good practice suggests that we should remember that disabled people are people first, and be more sensitive in the use of language; and that we are all dependent, to some extent, on assistance. Consideration of equal opportunities and disability legislation and ways in which disabled people may be empowered will help include disabled people.

Churches and other bodies need carefully to consider whether they unintentionally exclude people with disability. For example, someone with a wheat allergy or coeliac disease may not be able to participate in communion, and they are much less likely to feel 'different' or 'a nuisance' if everyone is given gluten-free bread. Similarly, someone with a tremor may be excluded from drinking wine from a chalicule (little glass) when a chalice might well enable them to take part. Similarly, the assumption that everyone will be able to hear without a microphone and the loop system 'because I have a loud voice' does not help people with hearing problems. Automatic provision or offers of transport may help those join in who would otherwise be unable to attend.

There is another debate which impinges on these issues but which opens up different pastoral and ethical considerations that cannot be taken up here. This is the right of people with degenerative, terminal illnesses to be assisted to commit suicide. On the other hand, many disabled and chronically ill people fear that such a law will either encourage people to ask for assisted death at a time when they are depressed, or will make others with degenerative conditions feel over-persuaded to end their lives so that they are not a nuisance to others or a cost on the health service. Alongside this is the argument that through palliative care it is possible to allow people to die with dignity.

Ageism

Ageism may happen not just because a person is considered to be too old, but because they are considered to be too young or too middle-aged. Newsagents who stop school children crowding into their shop, but let large numbers of adults in, may be acting from purely understandable motives, but this is an example of ageist behaviour. Much prejudice against young people is related to fear. Teenage lads who go around together wearing hoodies may be behaving in a purely reasonable way, but the size and appearance of the group may cause anxiety. Churches, too, must consider the needs of people of all ages. Some refuse to change traditional styles of worship. Those who say that children should not be present during the sermon, or become full members of the church, may be acting in an ageist way.

However, 'ageism' normally applies to old people. Discrimination is often based on the fear of being old or of dying. Job advertisements may suggest that only a young person should apply and, even if legislation makes such a practice illegal, employers may still select employees on ageist principles, especially in advertising or the media. Richard Hammond reports that 33 per cent would not interview someone over 70 because 'you do not have all your faculties'. Society, especially in the West, makes fun of those who are older. Look at birthday cards which emphasize negative and stereotypical aspects of ageing such as having wrinkles, being grumpy, or not being able to see or hear. While many may be lonely, as many lead busy lives and are happy to live on their own. It is widely assumed that older people must be asexual. Older women suffer from both ageist and sexist attitudes. Older people can also suffer because their needs do not appear to be 'sexy'. For example, the National Health Service spends more on expensive treatment for cancer or heart patients, leading to cost-cutting in geriatric medicine. Patronizing care workers can also encourage dependency rather than independency. Ageism can lead to violent abuse. Lucy Gannon's *Dad* sensitively showed how Dad's irritating and smelly habits created tension and then violence from his son. All of these situations can lead to a loss of self-esteem in older people, leaving them open to further discrimination.

Churches, however, have often been one of the few institutions which have naturally worked with all ages together, and some succeed at this very well indeed. The Russells have always taken their family to church with them and the children have befriended older people. Charlotte visited an elderly woman from the congregation, Phyllis, who had become more and more housebound. She used some of her pocket money to buy a muffin from a shop on the way home from school to share with Phyllis. When Phyllis died, Charlotte asked if she could read a poem that she had written about her at the funeral. The minister said that the poem had said more about Phyllis than all that he had to say. But, unfortunately, churches don't always succeed in ensuring a welcome. For instance, the Report *Ageing* quotes examples of churches which have changed the times of services so that older people do not now feel able to attend.

Current anti-discrimination legislation

Ageism is one of the last areas of equality legislation to be tackled by government legislation in the UK. Legislation implemented in October 2006 covers employment and vocational training for people of all ages. It means that churches and community organizations may no longer be able to insist that employees retire at 65 or a similar age.

Current legislation also includes the Equal Pay Act (1970), and the Sex Discrimination Act (1975) which make discrimination on the grounds of sex or marriage unlawful, together with the victimizing of anyone who takes such a case to court or a tribunal. However, it is not unlawful to discriminate against someone because they are not married. The Race Relations

Act (1976) outlaws distinction on the grounds of race, colour, nationality (including citizenship), or ethnic or national origin. Amended by the Race Relations (Amendment) Act 2000, it now includes public functions, even if those functions are carried out by a private business; and it also places a general duty on listed public authorities to promote race equality. The Disability Discrimination Act (1995) covers discrimination against disabled people. It originally applied to employers with 15 or more employees but changes implemented in October 2004 mean that it applies to most employers no matter how many members of staff. The Act is aimed to ensure that disabled people are not discriminated against for a reason related to their disability, including situations where, without justification, a 'reasonable adjustment' is not made. It also applies to the provision of goods, facilities and services for the public. The Employment Equality (Sexual Orientation) Regulations (2003) forbid direct and indirect discrimination, harassment and victimization in employment and training on the grounds of sexual orientation, and the Employment Equality (Religion or Belief) Regulations (2003) make similar provision in the area of religion or belief. Although the Human Rights Act (1998) is different from the other laws listed here, it is useful to know its basic provisions, as it is increasingly being invoked. There are 16 basic rights, from freedom from torture and killing to individual rights in everyday life. It also includes the right not to be treated differently because of race, religion, sex, political views or any other status, unless it can be objectively justified. It incorporates into UK law rights and freedoms guaranteed by the European Convention on Human Rights.

A biblical reflection on inclusivism

This is a central biblical theme. At the heart of the covenant given to Moses was the statement that the Hebrew tribes were rescued slaves, a cause for gratitude and humility. For that reason they were always to care for the stranger and the disadvantaged (Exodus 20.2; Leviticus 19.32–37), in a network of responsible and supportive relationships. It is clear that Jesus himself saw this as the mark of the Kingdom. He was a 'friend of tax collectors and sinners' including prostitutes (Matthew 11.19), of the sick and ritually unclean, touching and healing several lepers (Matthew 8.1–17; Luke 17.11–19). Are we as tolerant and unafraid when we meet people who are HIV positive or who have AIDS? There are, however, some issues here. Jesus heals, but we are not always talking about healing in the same way. Yet there is a real measure of healing, social and mental if not physical, in enabling the disadvantaged to enter more fully into the broader life of the community and in encouraging mutual support. Jesus himself clearly recognized the social implications by, for example, sending the leper to the Temple (Mark 1.40–45) and in his dealing with the woman who touched the hem of his garment (Luke 8.43–48). Ironically, today there might be some debate about whether or not to heal a deaf person if it means them being cut off from deaf culture.

With regard to disadvantages because of age there are two issues. First, the position of children. On the one hand the Bible refers to children as important to every family as a means to enable it to live on, but it gives fewer examples of the way in which children are valued for themselves. Children were to 'be seen and not heard', minors in the family, among the women. Yet Jesus valued them for their own sakes. 'Truly I tell you, unless you change and become like children, you will never enter the kingdom of heaven. Whoever becomes humble like this child is the greatest in the kingdom of heaven' (Matthew 18.3–4). Jesus blesses them (Mark 10.13–16).

Second, however, unlike our modern culture, the Bible shows how the elderly were valued in traditional society. In the wisdom literature, it is the elders who are the wise who govern the people and from whom the next generation should learn (Proverbs 1.8, 31.23). In 1 Timothy we see that the early Church followed the same custom. Timothy is told not to be afraid of his comparative youth as a leader in the Christian community (4.12) and he is urged to respect his elders (5.1–2). When choosing bishops and deacons one of the qualifications is their maturity and standing in the community (3.1–13).

This chapter has been concerned to indicate some of the key issues around discrimination and exclusion, especially as they have become increasingly shaped by a pluralist society. This affects every aspect of life, including the churches. It requires constant vigilance. The framework of law can set boundaries and to some extent shape behaviour; but, in the end, it is about repentance and inculcating generous and caring habits.

6

Working with allies

Churches and community projects do not have to struggle on alone to develop their work. There are many sources of help, advice and, sometimes, funding. Many of these have considerable resources compared to the congregation, though the churches often underestimate their strengths, from personnel to buildings. These include:

- statutory bodies such as social services, health care, police;
- the town hall, local councillors, planning units, co-ordinating committees for voluntary organizations;
- national voluntary agencies;
- funding bodies;
- regional and national church structures;
- other local community groups.

All will have expectations and will probably make demands. So this leaves churches and community projects with questions: who sets the agenda? When does collaboration become subservience? What kind of interdependence is needed?

David's story: starting from the bottom

When David came to be vicar of St Stephen's, Brighton Hill, an inner-city area of a large northern city, many people said that his task was hopeless. Perched on a hill in the centre of the parish was a large derelict Victorian church with a tall spire which could be seen all over the city; but the roof leaked, there were large cracks in many windows, and the church was dark and uninviting. The vicarage, a 1950s building next to the church, was also derelict. The few remaining members of the congregation said that as soon as they repaired the windows, young lads from the surrounding council estate threw more bricks through. The church was listed, so it could not be pulled down. What were they to do? Under David's guidance, the congregation began to think of new ways in which they could be church. Down the hill was a small shopping centre which still had some life in it. So the congregation decided to rent an empty shop. They spent some time brightening it up and providing central heating. The congregation moved from the church on the hill to the more cosy worship centre in the shop. A few more people joined them. There were a number of reasons: it was closer, warm, and more informal. Now the congregation could think what they could do about the building on the hill.

This required some research. Could it be of any use to the neighbourhood? If the building could be used, then how would they fund any work that needed to be done? They knew that their area was located in one of the most deprived areas in England, so they wondered whether they could work with the Neighbourhood Renewal Scheme. The whole idea sounded a little daunting, and David knew that very few of the present congregation had sufficient confidence or skills to find these things out. Would it be totally up to him, or could he find other support in the neighbourhood? He decided to talk to other church leaders and faith groups in the area. Sarah, priest-in-charge of St Werburgh's on the far side of the estate, Linda, the Brighton Hill URC's Church Related Community Worker, and the Catholic priest at St Mary's were all interested. Linda had already carried out a community profile of the area. She had also been networking with various other local voluntary community groups and had begun to make contact with the Local Strategic Partnership that had been set up by the local authority. This meant that she was able to give a lead when they began to look at the area as a whole.

The local authority

One of the first moves was to find out how the local authority and the statutory bodies might be willing and able to advise and support any projects.

Local Strategic Partnerships (LSP)

Churches and other voluntary and private sector bodies are being encouraged to be part of the decision-making process for local neighbourhoods. To this end LSPs had been set up over the past few years across England by the Government in the 88 most deprived local authority areas, of which Brighton Hill was one. They were entitled to receive additional resources through the Neighbourhood Renewal Unit Fund. An LSP is a single, non-statutory, multi-agency body, which matches the local authority boundaries, and brings together at a local level the public, private, community and voluntary sectors. They are regarded as key to tackling deep-seated, multi-faceted problems, and the range of responses that different bodies can offer together are likely to contribute to the successful redevelopment of the area. Rather than having planning decisions made by the local authority alone, they are now required to consult with local community and business groups about priorities and needs; this is to prevent what happened in another large city, where a private developer had negotiated with the council to pull down an estate that had been built cheaply in the 1950s and build an expensive mixed development for well-heeled city-dwellers. Little attempt had been made to listen to the existing residents who had been moved on to outlying council estates that themselves had a number of social problems; or some had been offered new social housing, but suspected that the rents would later be put up. The existing community had been totally broken up. So attempts were being made with LSPs to listen to local people. A combination of organizations and the community working co-operatively, so the theory went, would have a far greater chance of success. £182m. over five years (2001–06) had been provided nationally. Obviously not all groups or individuals could be represented on the executive board, but it was required to ensure that involvement and consultation were open to everyone and fed through to influence strategic plans.

Theory does not always work out in practice. It depends upon the involvement and engagement of those involved. Linda herself was the representative for the faith groups. This had enabled her to get to know the local Jewish synagogue and Hindu temple, as well as several local businesses and voluntary groups.

Brighton Hill was fortunate. Others, perhaps, with as great a need, for various technical reasons fall outside the boundaries of areas that are attracting special funding, whether national or from the European Union. This will make many tasks more difficult and complex. Nevertheless it is essential to get to know and to be known by a wide range of people in local government and the services that they provide. This will include the MP and/or Assembly member, the local ward counsellors and those that work on the patch in the statutory agencies, such as social work, health, the police, probation and education.

Voluntary work liaison structures

Most councils will have a mechanism for maintaining contact with the voluntary bodies in the area such as Voluntary Action Councils, designed to enable them to listen to the concerns of and to collaborate with the sector. It also allows members in the sector to find out what is going on and to benefit from each other's experience, to participate in training and receive regular briefings.

The planners and local development officers

Planning decisions have to be made in relation to the broader, strategic socio-economic policies of the borough as a whole. Thus it was vital for members of the group to talk to the city Planning Department. This produced a number of ideas for the development of both St Stephen's and the United Reformed Church's community centre. The local community could do with a large, comfortable hall to meet in. They also discovered that businesses were looking for a small, accessible conference centre with a café in which to hold training sessions. Several local artists were keen to find places where they could work and also display and sell their work. The idea began to form that they should create a conference and arts centre.

Local consultation

There is also another less formal level of consultation, but nonetheless important.

The church

The project forming at St Stephen's had arisen from the desperation of the congregation rather than a searching for ways to reach out to the neighbourhood. This inverts the normal pattern of working but probably represents the way many churches have moved into community activities. The first step often is to seek ways of funding the building through wider use. However, for this to be a sign of mission it cannot rest at the level of expediency. A genuine desire to be creatively participating in the life of the community must become part of the congregation's mentality. Such a conversion was, as we have seen, beginning at St Stephen's as the atmosphere changed from resignation to hope. It would be at that time that the process of auditing would be appropriate. Here, however, the Parish Audit had already been done by Linda.

Nevertheless there is another process that needs to be undertaken. The members of the church need to grow into the new vision and own it step by step. So there were regular meetings and news bulletins. It was here that a clash of opinions arose. Some of the congregation began to suggest that some of the more profitable suggestions were detrimental to serving the needs of a deprived community. Should they not rather be looking to provide workshops so that the unemployed can set up businesses, or build a new health centre, or provide youth work? The question would be how to finance such activities. It felt that they were being coerced by the city planners. In any case would not such plans effectively mean that St Stephen's was closed down? And how could it be seen as a positive Christian service? It was through such a debate, often sharp, that new possibilities emerged. It was possible to find a way, through sensitive adaptation of the site, to encompass both sets of requirements. At the same time, symbolically but importantly, a small worship or quiet area was incorporated and some modern artwork, depicting

Christian themes, was commissioned from a local artist. Also the pastoral care of those using the centre would be part of the brief of the local Churches Together.

Local people

Similarly it was important that local people should be informed and drawn into supporting a project that was of public importance. Too easily rumours circulate, raising unfounded apprehensions. It could look as though 'their church' was to be closed and sold off to the 'big boys'. How was this to be done? Public meetings are not always well attended or informative, though the one held proved useful as it drew together a number of key local people. But Linda also organized visits to the pubs, clubs, other churches, other faith centres, youth groups and bingo, even the mini-market where the Asian women tended to gather. Careful attention was also given to the community leaders, from the doctor to the police, from the newsagents to the postman. A number of other networks were picked up on. These activities stimulated greater awareness and hope in the residents, that something was happening in their community. The church was in the news. There were some significant offers of help, especially of practical skills. Moreover the churches learnt more about their community.

Drawing up plans and proposals

Building plans

The point came when they needed to draw up formal plans and proposals. To do this they needed professional help. Tom, the organist at the URC, happened to be an architect who was interested in urban regeneration and designed projects for church buildings, and he agreed to help draw up some plans for the new community and arts building complex, so that outline planning permission could be obtained.

However, Tom needed a detailed brief. For any plans to work there has to be a very clear idea how the building was expected to function; what activities were to take place; what facilities were going to be needed; and so forth. Tom had to listen to those who were instructing him; but it was also part of the learning process for the steering group. In dialogue they threshed out, as far as they possibly could on paper, what they wanted to happen to St Stephen's. This took a number of intense meetings. Then it came to the point when the plans were to be scrutinized by the congregation and other interested parties, and revised yet again. Meanwhile it was necessary to test the emerging proposals against the advice of the city planners. Eventually the plans were lodged with the Planning Office. After some months they were fully approved, giving the project five years within which to proceed.

At the same time it is also necessary to obtain parallel permissions from the ecclesiastical authorities. In this case it was the local Anglican diocese. Fortunately David found it easy to engage the bishop's interest in the vision. The diocesan architect was also supportive. With the help of the archdeacon all the requisite faculties were granted.

Funding

It was quite clear that a scheme was going to call for considerable funding. There was the capital funding for the buildings. This would have to be followed by the core funding for staff and maintenance, coupled with the income needed to set up and equip the different projects. Some income, it was hoped, would be obtained through rents and reimbursements from user groups, but that would only be after the initial outlay. The rest must be found. Early enquiries were a sensible precaution.

First, there were useful books indicating how to address the question and giving lists of trusts and other sources. The central library held many of these and also had an advice desk. David asked someone from the diocesan churches buildings advisory team to visit them to talk about the possibilities. The council will give advice, especially on local or Government funds. There are also the voluntary co-ordinating groups, set up by the council and others. It was worth St Stephen's paying subscriptions to one or two key bodies.

Should they apply for Lottery funding? The problem with this approach would be an ethical one. Their diocese had agreed that it was not ethical for churches to apply for a lottery grant for a project that contained a worship area. Some oppose using Lottery funding because people in disadvantaged groups spend precious money on Lottery tickets that might otherwise have been spent on rent or food. Others object because money goes to projects that should be funded out of taxation. A similar stance has been taken by, for example, the United Reformed Church. On the other hand, some believe that the good that may be achieved is a prior ethical imperative. In any case, they would argue, a refusal to use such funding is not an effective protest against raising money in this way.

There is, however, another issue, concerning the stipulations laid down by the granting body. It is always good to make sure that funder's requirements do not take you into ways of working that are not compatible with the values of the project. For example, some groups find that they have to take the word 'Christian' out of the title of their project. Some get over this by setting up a sub-group and giving it a non-Christian name. The issue is whether this is being as 'wise as serpents' (Matthew 10.16) or being deceptive. More and more, however, faith communities are encouraged to be partners in community renewal; though ironically it is sometime difficult to have a church so recognized; and there is the question of how and what kind of inter-faith partnership is expected.

David also contacted the Historic Churches Trust to try to obtain a smallish grant to help repair the roof. The Trust aims to ensure that churches and chapels remain open as places of worship and can only provide funds towards the maintenance of the ancient fabric.

Some entrepreneurial groups, such as Community Action Network (CAN), are springing up to provide expertise to local churches and community groups. David also discovered that this group might decide that, if the site really was not appropriate for a church or community centre, it might be more profitable to develop the site themselves, sell on for housing or office development and use the profit to grow or build a new church elsewhere. David also learned of a United Reformed Church in an immigrant area of a large city, which had grown to a major community resource that included a health centre and arts building. It had started by offering some local artists space on condition that they taught local people some of their skills. This led to an art course which is now validated by the local university. People with learning difficulties work on a garden around the project and in a café. A Methodist Central Hall had worked with city planners, in exchange for some of their land, to include a café, a centre for asylum-seekers, a catering business and a worship centre that was open to the new precinct. There seemed to be a number of avenues worth pursuing.

The business plan

Back in Brighton Hill David asked for advice from the local Treasure Chest Community Funders about the best way to make a grant application. He was told that they would need to produce a Business Plan. Information about writing a business plan can be had from different handbooks and packs such as the *Green Fish Factpack* (part of which is summarized below) and the URC *Assets for Life*. A Business Plan helps an organization to think through all aspects of their organization and plan for the future and is a useful tool for presenting their community project to funders and supporters. It should be clearly written, discussed with appropriate people and any costs indicated should be based on real costs. It should include the following:

1. a summary: one or two pages, summing up and introducing the project;
2. the background and history of your organization: this includes legal and charitable status, aims and objectives, and how managed; track record and achievements;
3. the needs: show a clear need and demand for the project, and evidence of research; emphasize the benefit of your project to the wider community;
4. aims and objectives: state your vision over the next three or five years, aims and outcomes;
5. workplan: list the tasks, when they will be done and who will do them (this will be used to monitor progress);

6 resources required: include staff, workspace and equipment and office costs, with a budget;
7 promotion and publicity: how you will advertize and target those you wish to reach, and promote yourself to supporters, partners, local churches etc;
8 management: job descriptions, responsibilities, supervision (the constitution should probably be given separately);
9 monitoring and evaluation: how you will measure success of your project.

The best business plans are a joint effort carried out by all the leaders and partners of the project. It can be an advantage to bring in a consultant, who may also produce the parish and church audits and open up contacts with appropriate statutory and other bodies. This can ensure a level of professional competence.

National local and voluntary agencies

Sarah, at St Werburgh's, decided to contact some national voluntary agencies to help her project of helping the homeless. Situated between a bingo hall and fast food restaurant, with a supermarket over the road in an inner-city urban priority area, the church had a congregation of about ten pensioners every Sunday morning. However, as it was on a patch that needed regeneration, the planners were looking hopefully interested in the area. Should St Werburgh's close and offer their land to developers, or should it do something to help the unemployed homeless people, some of whom sat in the church doorway sheltering from the rain? Sarah discovered that a local housing association, which was able to attract substantial grants from the local council, was looking for offices. The idea was born that these might be constructed in half of St Werburgh's, and the interior of the church might be brightened up for worship. The renovated church was now heated adequately and the meeting space that was created could be used by local groups, including Age Concern, as well as the housing association. The congregation grew. Eventually it was decided to use part of the graveyard for sheltered housing. Sarah was also able to work with a community centre for unemployed people and with a workshop which provided skills for local people selling reconditioned furniture. Sarah is now thinking about what mission might be possible to the local shopping street, working, perhaps ecumenically, with the City Industrial Mission. Working with voluntary organizations has certainly been a life-saver for the church, and it had also provided a means for the church to work with the local community.

It was a long haul, but it was certainly worth making formal and informal relationships with various other key persons and bodies in order to get their projects off the ground. Their churches were very much part of the community networks and, at the same time, they had found opportunity to make real contact with the people behind the desks who, as a result, saw the Church in a different light, allies with them in the difficult task of running a modern city, with their own strains and stresses. They frequently valued the informal chat over a cup of tea, and sometimes asked the leading question about faith and morality, exposing their search to make sense of it all. This really was witness and pastoral care.

7

Working with volunteers

Church congregations have perhaps more experience of voluntary service in the community than most organizations, but many have not moved on to develop a more professional approach to working. Yet church organizations that have embraced good practice are in the forefront of good community development. Thinking carefully about their recruitment and support is key. Happy volunteers stay. Projects also provide opportunities for both volunteers and users to develop their skills.

Rob's story – volunteers wanted

Rob is a Methodist minister working with a group of rural churches in south-east England in the Whaly Valley. When he arrived the population was mostly white, many from affluent backgrounds. Many commuted to London but some even, via Ashford and Eurostar, to Paris. Some of the village people did not willingly accept newcomers, even if they had been there for twenty years. Rob was thinking about how to tackle this situation, when the demographics changed dramatically. Asylum-seekers and refugees arrived, through Dover and Folkestone. Some were given casual work in the hop fields, orchards and packing industries.

Thus the churches were confronted with real life strangers. Reporters' articles reflected the exaggerated fear of newcomers. One immigrant, however, who had been in the UK for about five years, set up as a gang master to employ refugees workers on local farms. He had more English and money than most. He built hostel accommodation and hired vans to workers. In return for this, he imposed charges which left the others with very little. Many put up with this exploitative situation because they were illegal. The gang master, however, had not applied for planning permission, so the council informed him that his building would need to be removed. The gang master did not comply with their ruling. When it was demolished by force there were violent scuffles. Rob, who knew the gang master, was able to intervene and eventually the demolition went ahead reasonably peacefully. The result was that late that night, the council had more to re-house than they had anticipated. The minister volunteered to take them into the church hall, from which a large-scale project emerged to feed, shelter and find them work.

This did a great deal to bring the white population together. Rob and the church members had very little information, however, about the legal and practical aspects of looking after refugees. They sought advice from Kerry, a Church Related Community Worker, who worked in a local town with asylum-seekers and refugees. Kerry had been at Elm Park for some seven years. When she first arrived the church had a large, listed building and a small congregation. They gave away the large hall to a local group dealing with the elderly. The main building, though expensive to run, is still used occasionally for weddings and funerals. The smaller hall has been remodelled to provide catering facilities and for lets. The aim is for the building to pay for the upkeep of the church and its three full-time staff. The church now has a membership of 60, of all ages and cultures. The large number of activities based at Elm Park depend largely on voluntary help from church members and the community. It was some of the techniques that her church used to help encourage and develop volunteers that might be helpful to Rob and his churches as they struggled to support their refugee workers.

Preparing for volunteers

Additional help came from such organizations as the Churches Community Work Alliance (CCWA) the Federation for Community Development Learning, and the Shaftesbury Society, all of which regularly put on courses. Rob and a few representatives went on one. They visited Elm Park and Kerry visited Whaly Valley. Leaflets from varying local charities and council initiatives were displayed and experts invited to talk about such subjects as finding local employment and explaining something about the customs of living in Britain.

Recruiting volunteers

The Volunteering England website is a rich source of advice about recruiting and supporting volunteers. Getting the right people in sufficient quantities and retaining them is crucial. But before jumping into a recruitment campaign, it is essential first to ensure that any proposed project is well prepared. It is no good recruiting volunteers if there is no idea what their role will be, and how they will be selected and supported. Supporting volunteers is very important if they are to feel valued, an area that many churches are not good at. The key elements of support include a regular time to talk with each ('supervision'); work outlines (job description); discipline and grievance procedures and training. Selection could be an informal chat, but will need to be more formal if the role includes working with people, money or dangerous equipment. Selection will, as appropriate, include the use of application forms, references, interviews, criminal record checks (necessary for working with children and vulnerable people) and health checks.

Recruitment, even if using church members, will need some form of advertising, even if it is only verbal, and it is vital that there should be a clear message. This should include information about what the work is, what the organization does, and where to find out more. Think about the possible motivations for people to volunteer. Are they committed to your church or project? Then tell them the difference a volunteer can make. Do they want to meet people, or gain skills? If so, emphasize the opportunities for gaining skills and qualifications. Offer a taster session. Most volunteers are recruited through existing staff, clients, users, supporters or other volunteers, usually by word of mouth. Make sure that everyone knows that you are looking. Of course, happy volunteers are more likely to recruit others. But although this is the most effective method of recruiting, it is likely to recruit people who are similar to existing volunteers, which may end up with volunteers from a limited cultural and ethnic background.

Keep printed material simple, but with sufficient information. Posters, cards and bookmarks are helpful and may be left in churches and other religious centres, libraries, town halls and other public buildings, sports and leisure centres, shop windows and job centres. It might also be possible to run a volunteer day or to have a stall at a local fête. Information about your project can be released to the local press and radio. The *Guardian* newspaper runs a volunteers page every other Wednesday. There are also specialist papers such as the *Big Issue*, or the black press such as the *Voice*. Equal opportunity issues need to be kept in mind. Disabled volunteers, young people, older people, people from minority ethnic communities and unemployed people all have a great deal to give.

Induction of volunteers

Volunteers need to be inducted into your project and their role. Before they arrive they should have had basic information. Explain the goals of the project. Give a clear understanding of their role, including information about health and safety issues, first aid procedures, accident reporting, any policy on smoking, the emergency exits and evacuation procedures. They need to know how to claim expenses; what arrangements there are for personal support; the disciplinary and grievance procedures and details about training. Think about making induction more fun by using team exercises, visuals and opportunities for questions.

Training volunteers

The most common form of initial training is on the job, using a mentor for one or more working sessions. Volunteers can also be sent on training courses and those in the area will have to be discovered. If there are several volunteers, it is possible to try some in-house training, perhaps inviting an outside tutor, or making use of more experienced volunteers. Sometimes volunteers claim they do not have time for training and, anyway, it is not necessary. If so, has it been made it clear why training is important and what are the aims and objectives of any course? It also needs to be seen to fit their needs and to be at a time that they can reasonably manage.

Retaining volunteers

Volunteers are free to come and go. It is not, however, helpful to have a high turnover, nor for them to feel 'blackmailed' into staying because they believe that the organization will close if they leave. Some will start with enthusiasm but find the regular commitment difficult to sustain. There will always be changing circumstances and pressures that will make it hard to keep going. When Rob's project was first set up, people had been so angry that many members of local churches had jumped to join the rota to help. As time went on, however, several of them were less keen, claiming busy careers or families, and began to drop out. Rob understood how hard it was to keep on with a regular commitment. Without underestimating that, he felt something was needed to encourage them. Several lines of action occurred to him or were suggested.

The ministry of encouragement

As pastor, Rob tried to exercise a ministry of encouragement; that is, he listened to his people, supported them in their concerns but also reminded them of the grace of God that is there to support us. Attention was drawn to three biblical themes. First was the Parable of Wheat and Weeds (Matthew 13.24–30, 36–43) in which a farmer finds weeds among his crop. The servants want to pull them up, are told to wait because they might pull up the crop by mistake. This was seen to say, 'Don't be too quick to decide who you think are the outcasts in our society. Any task takes time before we see results. Things are much too complicated to make snap judgements.' Then there is the story of Barnabas, the Son of Encouragement. We don't hear much of him, but whenever we do, he's at somebody's side (Acts 9.27, 11.22–24). Paul, too, in 2 Corinthians 8—9, praises the Christians in Macedonia for their very generosity. These were the same people who were to support Paul in prison (Philippians 4.10–20).

Those who are relying on us need our perseverance, but this is also the way God deals with us.

Motivation

Think about what volunteers get out of their work. They may want to learn new skills or obtain work experience. They may have skills which they want to put at someone's disposal. They can have a special commitment to the issue that the project is addressing and so make a small but personal contribution. It may simply be that they want to feel useful, meet people, make friends and be part of a community. Few will stay long if they are not trusted or if the work is boring. Stuffing envelopes and photocopying alone will not encourage them to stay. Finding out how best to deploy and use their talents in worthwhile tasks is important. So is being part of a team in which everyone takes their responsibility seriously but also looks out for the others. Retaining volunteers is about relationships.

How to say 'thank you' to volunteers

Just saying the words, 'thank you' at the end of a session is important. Some community projects arrange special events to celebrate their volunteers' work, such as a meal, a social event, or even an award ceremony. It may be appropriate to contact the local media. People enjoy having their photograph in the local paper. There could be certificates. But it is best not to buy gifts for everyone because it creates expectations, unless, of course, there is a special occasion, such as someone retiring. A small gift such as a pack of seeds or a bookmark might be appropriate on other occasions.

These considerations prompted Kerry to suggest that the volunteers from the refugee project be nominated for the annual Pucktin award, named after a local hero. Each year the network for local community services held a special evening in a local theatre to give public recognition to the work of volunteers in the area. A local personality was invited to present a number of awards in nominated categories. That year, the Whaly Valley group won the best newcomers' category. This event proved to be very important for both thanking and also in keeping up the motivation of the volunteers.

Safeguarding vulnerable users

It is important that any organization that is working with children or vulnerable adults takes adequate care over the selection and preparation of volunteers. But even obligatory, enhanced-disclosure police checks only reveal past convictions and may not show up someone who might be a danger to others. All that most voluntary organizations can do is to follow thorough day-to-day good practice. Avoiding one-to-one contact between a volunteer and a vulnerable user helps protect both the user and volunteer. Good training is important to ensure that everyone is working in a culture of caring for the safety of users.

There may be a wish to consider recruiting ex-offenders. This is an important step in rehabilitation and follows equal opportunities good practice. Under the Protection of Children Act 1999 and the Criminal Justice and Court Services Act 2000, it is an offence knowingly to employ (paid or unpaid) anyone to work in a 'regulated position' with a conviction for crimes against children including murder, manslaughter, rape, GBH and a number of sexual offences. But there may be other situations. Consider such factors as whether the conviction is relevant to the proposed activity, the seriousness of the offence, the length of time since the offence, the circumstances surrounding the event, whether their behaviour is still a cause for concern, and the applicant's attitude to their offence. Take up references, but make sure that information is kept securely confidential.

Reprimanding a volunteer

One of the most difficult aspects of working with volunteers is disciplining them. They have given their time freely, so mentioning a problem is likely to be embarrassing. Many churches find that it is easier to put up with a difficult situation than to challenge it, but this is not helpful. The best method is to deal with the issue as soon as it becomes apparent, since, at this stage, it is generally possible to negotiate a change in behaviour. Issues that might need challenging include: persistently bad timekeeping, failure to respect confidentiality, taking on tasks outside the agreed remit, breaching health and safety regulations, misuse of the organization's equipment, theft, discrimination, or being under the influence of alcohol, drugs or some other substance abuse. As can be seen in Chapter 8, make use of an informal talk first. Only if this fails, move on to a written warning and dismissal, but allow for an appeal process.

Accreditation of voluntary work

Accreditation is the formal recognition of the achievements of an individual, linked to some internal or external standard. This can include confirmation of someone's previous experience and training, called variously accreditation of previous recognized experience and learning (APEL) or prior formal learning (APL). Normally this is recognized through the presentation of certified experience from working with a recognized and responsible body or a certificate or letter from an accredited body. Accreditation can help to provide motivation, increase skills, increase the likelihood of gaining paid work later, provide for personal development and provide a recognition of the contribution made to the organization. The temptation is to take volunteers for granted. In order for accreditation to be given by the project the volunteer must be performing specific tasks which demonstrate particular skills. Many community development accreditation routes are assessed using the key National Occupation Standards in community development training, produced by the Community Work Forum (2002): (See Figure 7.1). If volunteers are being encouraged to take courses, then the organization should be prepared to pay any costs. If, however, the volunteers themselves pay for NVQs etc., they are eligible to receive a tax refund. Grants may also be available from Learning Skills Councils, combining in 2001 the Training and Enterprise Councils and the Further Funding Council, who can also give advice on alternative sources of funding. Unemployed volunteers who are working toward an NVQ through their voluntary work should still be eligible for a Job Seeker's Allowance. External routes include:

Introduction

The key purpose of community development work is collectively to bring about social change and justice, by working with communities to:

- identify their needs, opportunities, rights and responsibilities
- plan, organize and take action
- evaluate the effectiveness and impact of the action all in ways which challenge oppression and tackle inequalities.

Key Role A:
Develop working relationships with communities and organizations

A1 Make relationships within communities
A2 Build relationships within and with communities and organizations
A3 Develop strategic relationships with communities, organizations and within partnerships

Key Role B:
Encourage people to work with and learn from each other

B1 Contribute to the development of community groups/networks
B2 Facilitate the development of community groups/networks
B3 Facilitate ways of working collaboratively
B4 Promote and support learning from practice and experience
B5 Create opportunities for learning from practice and experience
B6 Support individuals, community groups and communities to deal with conflict
B7 Take action with individuals, community groups and communities to deal with conflict

Key Role C:
Work with people in communities to plan for change and take collective action

C1 Work within communities to select options and make plans for collective action
C2 Contribute to collective action within a community
C3 Support communities to plan and take collective action
C4 Ensure community participation in planning and taking collective action
C5 Contribute to the review of needs, opportunities, rights and responsibilities within a community
C6 Work with communities to identify needs, opportunities, rights and responsibilities

(*continued*)

Figure 7.1 A summary of the National Occupational Standards in community development work key roles

Units imported from National Occupational Standards for Management.

Key Role D:
Work with people in communities to develop and use frameworks for evaluation

D1 Support communities to monitor and review action for change
D2 Facilitate the development of evaluation frameworks

Key Role E:
Develop community organizations

E1 Encourage the best use of resources
E2 Review and develop funding and resources
E3 Develop and evaluate a funding/resourcing strategy
E4 Develop people's skills and roles within community groups/networks
E5 Facilitate the development of people and learning in communities
E6 Develop and review community-based organizational structures
E7 Develop and maintain organizational frameworks for community-based initiatives
E8 Contribute to planning and preparation
E9 Co-ordinate the running of project
E10 Contribute to project closure

Key Role F:
Reflect on and develop own practice and role

F1 Identify and reflect on own practice, knowledge and values
F2 Review own practice, knowledge and values
F3 Evaluate and develop own practice
F4 Identify and take action to meet own learning and development needs
F5 Review and meet own learning and development needs

Figure 7.1 (*continued*)

- National Vocational Qualifications (NVQs);
- Open College Network (OCN);
- Foundation and BA degrees in Faith and Community Work (The Partnership for Theological Education, Manchester);
- Certificate in Interpersonal Skills for Volunteers (The Personal Development Unit, University of Wales, Lampeter);

• **Social justice:**	working towards a fairer society that respects civil and human rights and challenges oppression
• **Self-determination:**	individuals and groups have the right to identify shared issues and concerns as the starting point for collective action
• **Working and learning together:**	valuing and using the skills, knowledge, experience and diversity within communities to collectively bring about desired changes
• **Sustainable communities:**	empowering communities to develop their independence and autonomy while making and maintaining links to the wider society
• **Participation:**	everyone has the right to fully participate in the decision-making processes that affect their lives
• **Reflective practice:**	effective community development is informed and enhanced through reflection and action

Figure 7.2 Values of community development work

Source: Federation for Community Development Learning <www.fcdl.org/uk/publications/documents/nos/standards> accessed 19.11.06.

- ASDAN (Level 2) Certificate in Community Volunteering;
- TLS Lite (Training for Living and Service) Valuing Community (Community Work Desk, URC).

At the same time the list of core competences is useful as a guide to the kinds of training and staff development that may be done in house. To be recognized elswhere this should consist in clear recorded units of work externally assessed or sessions with a competent tutor.

Volunteers are the backbone of community work, a resource to be treasured and developed. This is even more true at a time when there are constant references to the difficulty of finding volunteers in many areas of community activity. Most church related activities are entirely run by such a dedicated band. It is part of ministry to care for them and to recognize their contribution. For full-time staff it is a significant part of their remit. The use and developing of volunteers may, incidentally, also be a source of income. Also, developing social capital is often written into the terms of grants and supporting volunteers is perceived as contributing to that aim.

8

The community leader

Church and community projects need to examine very carefully their understanding and practice of leadership to see if it is appropriate. This chapter, therefore, will be looking, albeit briefly, at a number of important issues:

- power and authority;
- leadership styles;
- collaborative working;
- staff development;
- dealing with conflict;
- the relationship between staff and users;
- the place and function of management committees.

Power and authority

Dan, a Church Related Community Worker, had just been appointed as leader to a large and expanding Church Community Project in a major city. Although he had some experience of being supervised himself, he knew that he would need to find out more about his leadership roles. He remembered from his college course that the misuse of power and authority is behind some of the difficulties that happen in church leadership, and that appropriate use of power is a useful way of helping teams achieve good work. He warmed to Tony Benn, when he said that he had five questions for people in power:

- What power do you have?
- Where did you get it from?
- In whose interests do you use it?
- To whom are you accountable?
- How can we get rid of you?

Most of us exercise power over others in some way or another, even if we are not aware of it, especially when we persuade others to do something for us. Charles Handy (1988, p. 68) had said that no power counts as power unless other people recognize it and that people's influence can vary in different situations. For example, a company boss who controls the company at work may come home to find that no one pays any attention to him.

Handy, also, identified a number of different kinds of power and argued that different power bases allow different methods of influence. *Physical power* is the power of people, such as bullies or physically big men who exercise superior force. Such an attribute might be useful to a bouncer at a nightclub and it might be useful in some jobs, such as that of a builder, but in most situations physical power is not especially helpful. On the other hand, it is noticeable that many people who are selected to be leaders happen to be tall.

Resource power is exercised by people who hold valued resources such as the treasurer, a grant-awarding body or those who may or may not recommend a pay rise or promotion. People who hold keys to the church buildings also have a kind of resource power.

Someone who holds a particular responsibility in an organization has *position power*, such as a minister, the project manager, or a local MP.

Expert power is exercised by people who hold important information or possess technical skills.

There is also *personal power*, the charisma exercised by certain people who have personalities that attract other people. This can be a very useful thing, provided that the person who exercises it also enables other people to own and participate in the vision. It needs to be exercised with humility as a servant ministry.

Negative power can be exercised by even the most 'powerless' of people, such as those who always respond to anything new with, 'We couldn't possibly do that.' 'We tried it before and it didn't work.' Similarly, there are people who stop progress by saying that 'Everyone thinks in this way', when, in all probability, only that person actually thinks like that. Handy says (1988,

p. 72) that 'outbreaks of negative power in an organization are symptoms of something deeper'.

Gatekeeper power is the power exercised by people who have information, but who might either pass it on or, on the other hand, block it. They judge what ought to be allowed. Dan could think of a number of ministers and church secretaries who blocked information by filing letters and leaflets in their waste-paper baskets.

There is also the power identified by Ivan Illich (Handy 1988, p. 74), *iatrogenesis*, the power exercised by people who consciously or unconsciously induce people to think that they only have the knowledge and skills for the situation. Professionals can be guilty of this. In other words the situation is set up in such a way that the powerful cannot be challenged and therefore are allowed to exercise power.

Everyone has power of some sort, though clearly power is not evenly distributed. There are those who can be called 'the powerful', whose position, authority, strength or knowledge gives them the advantage. Clearly, too, power can be abused, whether it be personal, corporate or state power. The weak can be oppressed and the powerful gain even more power. Yet power is a necessary part of life. Without it nothing would happen. Social structures depend on the exercise of power and authority to permit, command and restrain, to influence and carry out aims and objectives. Individuals, too, have power, both personally and as part of society, in order to live, work and participate in social existence. All power carries with it responsibility and the greater the power the greater the responsibility. As Tony Benn remarked, 'Who benefits at the expense of whom?' A careful watch has to be kept on the use and abuse of power.

Leadership styles

One's task as leader and the exercise of authority will depend on the nature of the organization involved. A number of different leadership styles have been identified, the main styles of which are set out in Figure 8.1 (overleaf). No one style is appropriate to every group and situation and different modes may be appropriate at different times and as circumstances change. If the building is

Authoritarian	Provider	Coaching	Consultative	Enabling	Delegating	Servant	Laissez-faire
3 types: 1 Leader announces his or her decision with no feeling of responsibility or accountability to share the reasons. 2 Leader announces his or her decision and shares the reasons behind it, which were prepared beforehand (monologue). 3 Leader presents decision and invites questions and clarification.	Used by people who see themselves as benefactors, providing for others. Hierarchical, helper–client donor–beneficiary	The leader continues to direct and closely supervise tasks but also explains decisions, asks for suggestions and supports.	**3 types:** 1 Leader presents decision and invites questions of clarification. 2 Leader presents situation, gets input and makes decision. 3 Leader calls on members to make decision but holds veto.	**2 types:** 1 Leader defines limits, calls on members to make decision. 2 Leader calls on members to identify limits, explore situation, and make decision.	The leader turns over the responsibility for decision-making and problem-solving to subordinates. Making collective decisions.	The servant leader inspires others to achieve goals by serving them.	Leader has casual, easy-going style.
Jesus' style of Leadership							
Cleansing of the temple: Matthew 21.12–17; Mark 11.15–19; John 2.13–25 Jesus and Peter: John 21.15–19		Preparing for Passover meal: Matthew 26.17–25; Mark 14.12–21; Luke 22.7–13	Temptations Luke 4.1–13	The woman who anointed Jesus: Matthew 26.6–13; Mark 14.3–9; John 12.1–8	Sending out the disciples Matthew 10.5–15; Mark 6.6b–13; Luke 9.1–6	Jesus pours water into a basin and washes the disciples' feet (John 13.3–9).	

Figure 8.1 Leadership styles

L. Husselbee: adapted from Hope, Anne and Timmel, Sally, *Training for Transformation*, p. 102.

on fire, then survival will demand an *authoritarian leadership*. On the other hand, if working with people with the aim of helping them develop maturity and responsibility, then an *enabling* or *consultative style* is appropriate. Alternatively, working with a group of young people who resent any kind of authority, such as might be encountered by detached youth workers, a permissive or *laissez-faire* approach might be most appropriate. Part of the art of leadership is to recognize what is appropriate at any given moment. However, it is always vital that it affirm and value the people with whom the leader is working.

A biblical comment

What are the qualities and perspectives that would be underlined as key in a Christian perspective? Does faith make any difference?

The basic source for reflection must be the Bible and especially the life and teaching of Jesus. Clearly the central image is that of the servant, with which Jesus identified himself, and which was to become so important for the Church (Matthew 20.20–28). But what does this mean? That the leader should be a doormat, at everybody's beck and call? Surely not. Of course there is the commitment to be there for the good of the project, for the users and for the team; but that involves taking up the responsibilities and tasks that have their own leadership demands, exercising judgement and discernment and sometimes taking hard decisions. It means being able to initiate as well as to respond, to resist as well as to agree, to confront as well as to support. Serving is doing the task given.

There are other images in the Scriptures which can also inform our perception of leadership. A number of these are about caring. The shepherd lives with and defends the sheep (John 10.1–21); but there are also pictures of parenting, both of mothers and fathers (Isaiah 49.15f, 66.13; 1 Thessalonians 2.7, 11; Luke 12.30–32) and of building (1 Corinthians 3.10–15). Leaders, too, are expected to set the direction like a pilot (1 Corinthians 12.28, translated 'administration'); or to diffuse conflict by exposing themselves like a fool (1 Corinthians 4.10–13). The leader has to be in training like an athlete (Philippians 3.12–16), developing personal qualities such as endurance or perseverance (Galatians 5.22), integrity, honesty and credibility (1 Timothy 2.2), and humility (1 Peter 5.5), which includes being able to acknowledge mistakes and failure (1 John 1.8–10). Above all there are the resources of grace through the Holy Spirit to strengthen and support (Ephesians 5.13–18).

Dan, to sum up, could only come up with an idea of 'vocation'. This was not construed in terms of absolute certainty or sudden decision, but as a quiet conviction that he is in the right place at the right time with a worthwhile job which he can do well. This injects a quality to his work that lifts it above a mere task or a means of earning money. It is valuable in itself, as are the relationships within it.

There is here, however, a real danger of not recognizing one's limitations and vulnerability. As with pastoral ministry, the church-related community worker is a representative person of the Church and all that it stands for. The temptation is to try to be perfect, not to let any defect show, nor to let the side down by failure. At the same time caring for others can lead to stress and burn-out. But part of the reality of faith is to accept failure and weakness, that one is accepted in the beloved (Ephesians 1.6); also to acknowledge the need for support. After all the life of the Body of Christ is, or should be, a mutual sharing (1 Corinthians 12).

Maslow's hierarchy of needs

At the heart of leadership there has to be the ability to work with others so that they feel affirmed and appreciated. It may be instructive, therefore, to turn to the classic exploration of human social behaviour, Abraham Maslow's theory of 'the hierarchy of needs', to reinforce this point. He argues that people are motivated as a result of the imperative to satisfy various kinds of needs. At the most basic level we all have physiological needs such as food, drink and sleep, which are about basic human survival. Close behind these come the basic need for 'security', safety and shelter. So a personal assistant, who had been asked to leave her flat, found that she could not really settle to her work while she was looking for new accommodation. People in church or community who are without shelter and who have little money for food are unlikely to be concerned about faith development. Maslow then went on to define a number of higher needs, which, he believed, influence the behaviour of people at work. He divided them into three groups:

1 social needs:	sense of belonging social activity affection (love)
2 self-esteem needs:	self-respect status esteem of others
3 self-fulfilment needs:	growth personal development accomplishment creativity

He suggests that if social and self-esteem needs are not met the employee will exhibit one or more of: aggression, non-co-operation, apathy or alienation. If these needs are met but self-fulfilment is not, then the employee will merely do the job adequately but without enthusiasm. If all three are met, Maslow says, the employee will exhibit motivation and a creative interest in the work. Other researchers have added that a lack of opportunity to satisfy some of the higher needs can lead to stress and ill-health. This can be observed both on the shop floor and in the boardroom. Interestingly, one of the most important features of Maslow's theory is that once a need is satisfied it is no longer a motivator. There must be the opportunity to strive to satisfy a higher need if the employee is to continue to be anything more than passive.

So what relevance does this have? The person who is entering on to a piece of work needs to feel a sense of belonging, to know what is expected from them, and that they will be consulted about aspects of the job. Knowing where to obtain stationery or how to work the photocopier is important for those who need these facilities, as is an adequate induction for a new churchwarden, elder or deacon.

It also helps for workers to meet alongside the job, such as eating their sandwiches together or, occasionally, going for a meal. Taking a group of workers out to a retreat centre for a day or two to discuss future vision is also very effective. This, together with creating a relaxed and friendly atmosphere, will enable people to feel part of the group and not just an individual working on their own.

Leaders who have gained most respect take an interest in people (however junior they might be), considering that they will have something to contribute, praise people, when this is appropriate, and give support when someone is experiencing difficulties. Delegation also strengthens the worker's self-esteem. Destructive criticism and lack of recognition will reduce the self-esteem and status of a worker. Effective leadership means giving time. Rushing around doing important business but with no time for people may not be what is intended, and often merely dispirits others. It is also important to meet personal self-fulfilment needs (Chapter 9). A self-development plan should exist for all paid workers, and it is no bad idea to include volunteers.

Collaborative working

Belbin team roles

Teams have a number of primary and complementary roles that must be fulfilled if the necessary tasks are to be carried out. Belbin examined the characteristics of teams of managers on a training exercise, and discovered that successful teams were made up of people who were able to make sure that eight basic roles were carried out in the team. These are set out on Figure 8.2. A team with too many people who wanted to be in charge and too few people to actually do the work would not be helpful. Someone has to come up with new ideas; someone has to diffuse conflict or tension; someone has to analyse; someone has to look after the tasks that need to be done, such as writing the minutes; perhaps someone has to challenge the rest of the team.

Malcolm Bird (1992, p. 52) suggests that good teams should have: a definable membership; a shared sense of purpose; group pride; a clearly visible interdependence; much interaction between the members; a climate where the group works as a single organism; and most of all, members who want the team to succeed.

Overall	Belbin roles	Description
Doing/acting	Implementer	Well-organized and predictable. Takes basic ideas and makes them work in practice. Can be slow.
	Shaper	Lots of energy and action, challenging others to move forwards. Can be insensitive.
	Completer/Finisher	Reliably sees things through to the end, ironing out the wrinkles and ensuring everything works well. Can worry too much and not trust others.
Thinking/ problem-solving	Plant	Solves difficult problems with original and creative ideas. Can be poor communicator and may ignore the details.
	Monitor/Evaluator	Sees the big picture. Thinks carefully and accurately about things. May lack energy or ability to inspire others.
	Specialist	Has expert knowledge/skills in key areas and will solve many problems here. Can be uninterested in all other areas.
People/feelings	Co-ordinator	Respected leader who helps everyone focus on their task. Can be seen as excessively controlling.
	Team worker	Cares for individuals and the team. Good listener and works to resolve social problems. Can have problems making difficult decisions.
	Resource/investigator	Explores new ideas and possibilities with energy and with others. Good networker. Can be too optimistic and lose energy after the initial flush.

Figure 8.2 Belbin team roles

Source: <http://www.belbin.com/belbin-team-roles.htm>

Personality tests and teams

Some teams, in order to assess the personal qualities of their members, have made use of such tests as Myers-Briggs Type Indicators and/or the Enneagram.

If a team is interested in trying out a Myers-Briggs Personality Indicator exercise or any other such test, it is necessary to find a trained operator. Unskilled use of the methods or discussion of the findings could lead to dangerous consequences. Those teams that have tried this have, however, in the most part, found it to be useful (unless of course, individual members of the team have the type of personality that does not regard such tests as being useful!).

The relationship with other members of the team

Before he had begun working for a church project, in the voluntary sector, Dan had worked in business in a firm where everyone was paid and there was a hierarchical structure of line management. Working in the voluntary sector (and in particular for the Church) meant that relationships between various paid and unpaid colleagues did not work in this tidy fashion, not least because leaders in the church did not perceive the culture of working for the church as being in any way similar to that of business. Moreover there was the position of the volunteers. They frequently selected themselves and, once in place, even if their work was not helpful to others, they were difficult to remove. Some volunteers exercised considerable informal power over others despite the fact that they had not been given this authority. On the other hand, the people he worked with now genuinely wanted the best for those for whom they worked, and a friendly atmosphere.

Relationships between ministerial colleagues

As this is a church-based community project Dan will have to work closely with the minister, and less closely with others in neighbouring churches. Many ministers tend to work as lone individuals and do not easily fit into collaborative working. On the other hand, there are teams of ministers who have a good working relationship. Also, leadership styles tend to vary from one denomination to another, with one style predominating in any one case, although, in practice, there can be a wide variety in any denomination. So, for example, Anglican priests are expected to take a strong lead and to chair such meetings as the board of governors of the church school and various parish committees. They have pastoral and administrative responsibility to the bishop for all that goes on in their parish. On the other hand, denominations which adopt a congregational and more democratic method of making governance, such as Baptists, Congregationalists and the URC, are often more collaborative. The Board of Elders administers the affairs of the congregation, responsible to the Church Meeting of all members. This does not mean that the minister does not have considerable power, and presides over various meetings, which sometimes leads either to an underuse or an overuse of power. These historical and cultural differences can lead to difficulties in ecumenical co-operation, which, happily, is beginning to break down as the churches more and more see each other as partners.

Another issue is the relationship between different ministries. Several factors come into play. Some denominations are more hierarchic, though even where there is meant to be parity of ministry, such as between the minister of Word and Sacrament and the Church Related Community Worker in the URC, the former frequently is given precedence. This can sometimes lead to the anomaly that the minister is chair of the Management Committee. This should not happen. It is better for a suitable lay person to take that role, and for the working relationship to be carefully worked out. There can also be a tension between paid and unpaid ministries, even though they are each fully recognized. Last, there is the difference between ordained and lay ministries, the latter of which are not always adequately affirmed.

All these tensions can be found in the area of management of church-related community work projects. Not only is there a more informal style that tends to mark voluntary bodies, but there are also the different management styles in the various churches, which is different again from community work practice. Those likely to be employed will themselves probably have had a very different training and experience, possibly from business or industry but more likely from one of the caring or educational professions, as well as from community work. This confusion of backgrounds can lead to misunderstandings and frustration. It is also noticeable when one of the management committee brings with him or her both professional and church experience and is not sure which one to bring into play. But where the project is dealing with large sums of money, agreed and acceptable structures have to be set up and lines of demarcation and responsibility clearly acknowledged.

Relationships with the other officers of the congregation

Tensions can also emerge if the officers of the church assume that they can exercise authority over the centre manager or impose their style of doing things. This is compounded if employees of a community project do not communicate adequately back to the church and its officers. This is particularly true when different timescales apply. Community projects often have to work fast and make decisions quickly while, traditionally, churches can take months to come to a decision. For example, Mary, a centre manager, had obtained a substantial grant from the Lottery to improve the toilet area in the church, but had to spend the money within two months. The church officers naturally wanted a say in the way in which their toilets were improved, and wanted the issue to be debated by various elders' and church meetings, which would take making the decision well beyond the deadline. One of the church officers became very angry with Mary for going ahead without sufficient consultation. Such tensions might have been avoided if the project had authority for making such decisions, at least within acceptable limits, as part of its standing orders. At the same time, the church officers could have been more flexible, holding an emergency meeting before the deadline. Or should Mary, perhaps, have consulted before she applied for the grant? Alternatively, are some grant offers with too many difficult conditions best refused?

Relationships between volunteers and paid employees

Similarly, misunderstandings can emerge between volunteers and paid employees when expectations of how they work are markedly different. Employees may expect that their working hours are regulated and that they are entitled to adequate time off. Volunteers may be critical of employees taking time off when they give all of their time 'for free'. Volunteers, on the other hand, may adopt a casual attitude to the work, arriving late and leaving early without negotiation because family requirements have cropped up. This can annoy paid workers who are depending on them to cover their time allotment or complete a piece of work. There is no reason why volunteers should not expect to be available for certain agreed hours. It also helps if employees and volunteers have the opportunity to make decisions together, listening to one another's concerns.

Working collaboratively in a rural setting

Rebecca had just been appointed as rector within a rectorial benefice of eight Anglican churches in a rural area. She had been asked by her bishop to form an effective team with the two other stipendiary priests, one non-stipendiary priest and three lay readers who worked within the group. Previously there had been very little collaboration. The two stipendiary priests, both nearing retirement, had been used to working on their own with very little contact with other clergy in the area. They had felt threatened by the newly trained non-stipendiary minister and the lay readers. There were also two Methodist, one Baptist and one United Reformed churches in the area, with whom Rebecca wanted to work.

The area showed all the symptoms of contemporary rural life. Congregations were small, but it would not be a solution to amalgamate them as each was central to their village community. There was expensive housing, occupied for the most part by people who worked in London and nearby cities. There was, however, also considerable poverty. The price of housing meant that young adults were forced to live with their parents, even after marriage. Some people could not now afford to run cars and were dependent upon the infrequent bus services. Many did not go out after dark and were very isolated as a result. Only some of the villages had a shop or pub. Some old people were frightened by youths who met to take drugs under a local bridge.

The clergy would need to work together collaboratively if they were to face up to many of these problems. The first thing that was needed was for the leadership team of the churches to spend time together getting to know one another. A church training officer was brought in to help them. Although one thought that this would be a waste of time, the others were elated to be given time out. Before this they had not felt particularly valued, but this helped them to feel that they were members of a team. This was particularly true for the readers and non-stipendiary minister. They began their day together with team-building exercises. This enabled them to get to know each other. They then looked at key team roles. After lunch, they began to discuss some of the issues that were important for their area. It was agreed that they would meet together once a week for prayer and to plan a programme for the week and to meet for a whole day once a quarter. Rebecca also visited each member of her team regularly, a relaxed and informal form of supervision. Gradually, a sense of team developed, and its members began to pick up in enthusiasm.

Out of this process came the decision to apply to employ a detached youth worker, to set up a 'library' of donated books in one of the churches, and a 'good neighbours' scheme for the increasing number of the housebound. They also looked into the local council's proposal for a new estate of 200 houses, concerned that no community space or shop was planned. How, too, could the Church have a presence in this new area?

Communication

Effective communication between the members of the team and the churches would be crucial if everyone were to feel involved. Previously, each of the churches had their own news-sheet or magazine. It was suggested that they should produce a group magazine each month, which would have space for individual church news but also to publicize their projects and be a forum for local concerns. This would be less work than producing a magazine for each and, together, they might be able to afford a better quality of production. They also decided to take a fresh look at their church notice boards. Many of them gave the impression that the churches were no longer functioning. It would also be useful for a group to go round each of the churches to assess their appearance and impact. They might also have a joint bonfire party to burn some accumulated hoards of rubbish. Posters advertising events should be attractive, including Christmas cards for each household.

Collaborative styles developed across the board. The URC elders began to meet more frequently, sometimes with the churchwardens and the Methodist steward. The readers and lay preachers were encouraged to attend meetings with the full-time clergy by better timing. The priests and ministers further decided that they could support one another by having co-appraisal sessions once a year. This would relate to the Anglican appraisal set up by the diocese and the Accompanied Self-Appraisal systems of the Methodists, Baptists and URC.

Caring for people and the organizations

Working professionally

This means, first of all, attention to all the responsibilities and legal obligations demanded in modern management. It is almost impossible for one person to encompass the range of skills and information required. This is why projects need every bit of help they can get, which includes the resources for training available from the local area and national bodies and the considerable literature. Some projects obtain some of this support by partnerships with specialist bodies. Many bring on to their boards volunteer experts, accountants, lawyers and human resource managers. These responsibilities range from hiring and firing, to equal opportunities, finance, taxes, disability, racial and other good practices, protection of young people (see Chapter 5), health and safety and grievance procedures (see Chapter 7). All this is not just for legal reasons but for the good image of the project and the protection of workers and clients. The project would be compromised if there were any inappropriate behaviour not addressed seriously. People accessing and funding the services need to be able to rely on its integrity.

Supervision

One of Dan's new workers asked him when she arrived what the arrangements were for supervision. She explained that in her previous work it was very difficult to discover what was expected of her because her boss never set aside time to talk to her. This led to uncertainty and dissatisfaction. This is not an infrequent experience, not least in voluntary organizations. She was assured that here the proper structures were in place.

It is necessary to overcome a certain suspicion of supervision. In church circles it is sometimes claimed that 'business' techniques, with line managers and appraisal are inappropriate. It smacks too much of hierarchy. There is also a fear of judgementalism. However it is important to see that a technique is an instrument that can be used or abused. Properly understood, supervision is a way of regularizing something that should be happening anyway. It may not be so important in small groups that regularly confer and support one another; though this equivalent is often missing. But in larger contexts it is a way, first, of ensuring that there is regular contact between those that are responsible to each other; second, it is a pastoral opportunity for checking up on how the job is going; third, it is a chance to look at the future and where the job and supervisee are going; fourth, it is a recognition of obligation to the project as a whole. It is thus for the good of both the employee and the enterprise (Adirondack 2000, p. 121).

Dan, having allayed the anxieties of some, set up a pattern whereby he would see the full-time staff monthly for an hour or so, and the volunteers every eight weeks. There is a value in timetabling these sessions because, if they are not in the diary, they can easily be brushed aside by more pressing engagements.

Preparing for the supervision session

A supervision session itself could just be a general chat with a colleague about how things are going. But those sessions that are most useful are the ones where there has been some preparation beforehand in response to some questions. Thus Dan asked his workers to answer the following questions:

1. What has gone well? What things, since the last session, am I particularly pleased about?
2. What things am I unhappy about? Why might things have gone wrong? What could be done to prevent this happening in the future, or how might things be improved?

3 Are there any things that are causing me stress? Is there anyone creating a problem for me?
4 Have I achieved what I set out to achieve since the last session?
5 What do I hope to achieve in the next month/six weeks/year?
6 Are there any courses or training events that might improve my work and be of benefit to me personally in the future?

In turn, the supervisor would think about the following questions before the session:

1 What has the worker/volunteer done since the last session that I am particularly pleased about? How has the work improved? What might have made the work even better?
2 Is there anything that I am unhappy about? How did it happen, and could it be prevented in future?
3 Has the worker done what was agreed at the last session and am I satisfied with the quantity and quality of the work? Does the worker seem to be overworking or underworking? Is his or her timekeeping good?
4 What work might he or she concentrate on between now and the next session?

The questions suggested for the supervisor to think about are often frowned on in church circles, but expected in the community development field. It is important for the supervisor to approach the session not in a culture of blame but, at every point possible, in a culture of praise. Above all, it is very important for the supervisor to listen to what the worker has to say. If it is necessary to point out a problem, then this needs to be done sensitively. It is important not to say later that what had been said was a verbal warning unless this has been made clear at the time. There should always be an agreed memo of the conclusions of a session for both parties. It is sometime necessary to refer back to these, both to note progress and to be reminded of what was said, especially in case of dispute.

Appraisals

Supervision sessions deal with the day-to-day work, whereas appraisals are designed to take a more long-term view. They are more concerned with personal and career development and devising work goals and objectives for the next year or so. Most usually appraisals take place a few weeks after a person starts work, then (if there is a probationary period) after six months, and then at the end of a year. Thereafter, they generally take place once a year and are led by senior management. One person in the organization is generally responsible for keeping track of the appraisal process. This would normally be expected for each full-time member of staff, but should include part-time staff and, certainly if desired, volunteers. Up until recently, there was no real appraisal system for ministers and other church employees. Increasingly, however, churches have been setting up schemes, initially not compulsory; but recently this has begun to change. For example, the URC General Assembly (2006) decreed that appraisals should be compulsory for ministers and Church Related Community Workers. Most ministers' self-appraisal schemes are less frequent than every year. Ministers are usually asked to complete a questionnaire about their current work, their joys and disappointments, visions for the future, personal faith development and what would be valuable in future training.

Support groups and mentors

Dan was also interested in promoting other important ways for those working in his centre to receive support.

First, there is another understanding of supervision. This is to have what can be termed a consultant supervisor. This is someone detached from the day-to-day working situation who acts as a sounding board against which to check out personal practice and with whom to clarify personal issues. This would be expected in any counselling service. Individually or in small groups counsellors can, in a safe and confidential environment, reflect on their engagement with their clients. Perhaps this should be more usual in community work. It is, of course, possible to set up such an arrangement privately. It is best between two people who are comparative strangers and under a clear contract. In other contexts such a person might be called a spiritual director or soul friend.

Second, especially where working alone, it is valuable to have a small 'support group'. This may be three or four persons who are interested in the project and can bring to bear some expertise, to act as a think tank independently of the formal management structures, though its existence is known to the management committee. In a church setting this is a way, through suitable appointments, of having a cross link between the community work and the congregation.

Third, there are various teams and networks. In the workplace the team itself should be the primary source of support, both formally through team meetings, away-days and so forth, and through the camaraderie built up over time, which takes the strain in difficult times. But there are a number of variations on this theme. Dan and his full-time workers were members of several professional bodies, nationally and locally. This could include the Churches Community Work Association and the Voluntary Action Council's city-wide forum. Here they are able to meet others in community work, exchange news and share best practice. At another level, it is possible to be part of a loose framework that links together a range of community-related professionals in the locality, sharing concerns and collaborating as necessary. For the lone community worker this is probably a necessary lifeline.

It is valuable to remember that there are networks, detached from the day-to-day business, that can be drawn on. This could be the Round Table or the close group of friends that frequent the same pub regularly. For the Christian there are such scattered communities as the Iona Community, the Franciscan Tertiaries or Focolare.

Faith development

For the Christian, not least those whose work is regarded as part of the witness of the Church, it is important to grow in Christian understanding and wisdom. It is too easy to be professionally sophisticated but remain stuck in matters of faith. There should be a clear commitment to learning more about the Christian faith and its relevance to community activity. This is one of the key competences required of the Church Related Community Worker in the URC. There are two interlocked activities. First, there is the need to acquire greater knowledge about the foundations and doctrines of the faith, through reading, taking courses, attending conferences, included as a regular component of study and study leave. Then there is the need to reflect theologically on the work (see Chapter 9). It is best structured so that it becomes a regular part of the rhythm of life. It could take the form of a journal or as part of the supervisory process or in team meetings. Or, outside the system, there could be a group to belong to, or membership of a house or prayer group. In this way there is opportunity for the four elements to interact, professional practice, theological insights, daily experience and one's inner journey.

A biblical note on mutual support

Paul's letter to Philippi is one of the most personal, revealing the Apostle's inner thoughts and his relations with what surely must have been his favourite congregation. We find a deep respect and mutual affection. The Philippians owe their Christian existence to Paul and value his loving care. Paul is grateful for, indeed dependent on, their generosity (2.25–30, 4.15–19). They worry about each other, now separated, a situation made worse by Paul's imprisonment. Faith holds us together in love so that we are open to each other's needs. At the same time there is a constant note of joy (1.18, 2.18, 28, 3.1, 4.4, 10). This is not glib but a deep sense of trust that the darkness is not the final word, even if the future is unknown. Joy is the expression of their commitment to Christ that undergirds Paul as he pursues his calling, wherever that may lead him (3.2—4.1). Faith is in God, not our own assets or capabilities. In Christ we can find a well of resource, the reality within which our lives are set. This is the way of triumphal paradox (4.11–14). This is not suffering for suffering's sake but a willingness to accept the responsibility and discipline of the task undertaken. So it can end with a note of confidence and praise (4.19–20).

Dealing with conflict

In any group or organization there will be different points of view, priorities and aims. If these differences can be discussed and alternative views respected, a healthy working relationship can exist. If, however, differences cannot be satisfactorily dealt with, then conflict can arise. This may reflect deep-seated disagreement about standards or values. It may also arise if something such as pay, expenses, responsibilities, status or workload is seen as unfair. Others may feel that they are being bullied or that some people are exercising undue and unfair power. Again it may be a matter of a reluctance to consider change or a lack of trust in colleagues. Many groups (and many church or voluntary groups fall into this category) find it very difficult to deal with conflict. People may pretend that the conflict is not happening or hope that the problem will go away. Conflict that has not been resolved is likely to fester and keep resurfacing, often in ways completely unrelated to the real problem. Conflict may be painful to deal with but it is nearly always worse in the long run to pretend that it is not there.

Most day-to-day conflicts can be resolved by the group themselves, but if it becomes more serious, then a third party may need to be brought in. There are a number of processes which are available to help control and then resolve conflict.

1 Crisis intervention: by separating or protecting people, getting help, intervening in a situation that is likely to get heated, giving people a chance to calm down (Adirondack, p. 139).
2 Facilitation: a facilitator helps people to listen to and communicate with each other.
3 Conciliation: this is the process of working towards a reconciliation, not necessarily with a third person.
4 Mediation: conciliation with an intermediary.
5 Advocacy: an advocate supports or negotiates on behalf of one party.
6 Negotiation: discussing each party's needs, demands and interests and agreeing which aspects should be incorporated in a solution.
7 Arbitration: a legal (or quasi-legal process) in which the parties beforehand agree to accept the decision of the arbitrator.
8 Adjudication or litigation: settlement of a dispute using formal legal processes.

Whichever is used, it is important for each party to have an opportunity to put their side and to clarify and define the issues as they see them. Each party also needs to be given the opportunity to say what they want to be done about a situation. It helps, too, if common interests and goals can be identified. This, hopefully, leads on to defining, discussing and agreeing a solution which both parties are willing to implement. It is also helpful to work out a procedure for reviewing the situation some time later to see whether the solution is working.

Suppression may be appropriate in minor conflicts where people do not care much about the outcome or where it does not affect people's work, but not just to 'keep one happy family'. In situations where power is unevenly distributed, someone down the hierarchy may not think that there is any point in trying to challenge someone much higher up who could make life very difficult. In the end, however, they will have to decide whether to live with the situation or to get out if they are not to suffer considerable stress. Talking the issue over with a third (neutral party) would be very helpful. There are occasions when decisions are taken by people who do not really have the right to impose them, including conflict issues. In such cases, any conflict is unlikely to be resolved. Neither denial, suppression nor imposed solutions are likely to get to the root of the problem. That requires everyone to discuss, negotiate and to come to a jointly agreed solution through a process of compromise or consensus. For this to work, all parties must want to find a solution, be willing to argue rationally and to be willing to listen. They must also be willing to entertain a range of solutions and be willing to accept a compromise. Sometimes just hearing where they are coming from is enough to resolve the situation. If there is a forum where different views may be discussed and where people can listen to one another with respect, it is less likely that conflict will arise, especially if everyone feels that they have a say in decision making.

The relationship of the workers with the users

A further relationship that the community leader needs to be concerned about is that between the workers in a project and the people who make use of the project. The first requirement is that those running and working for the project are appropriately skilled. Some fairly basic skills will be required by workers to enable them to listen and appreciate the experiences of those whom they are helping, although the leaders will need to be aware of the kinds of graver and technical issues that need addressing with this group. On the other hand, if the project is set up to provide skilled services of one kind or another, such as counselling, then considerably more skills are required by all those concerned. In this case organizations such as Cruse Bereavement Care or the Samaritans will provide a careful selection process for volunteers and will give training. Those who are to provide more in-depth counselling will need to undertake at least a two-year course and receive counselling themselves. It is very important that well-meaning volunteers do not try to help others beyond their area of expertise, and know when to refer people on to a better qualified worker or indeed to other more qualified groups.

It can be very tempting for workers and volunteers to believe that they make decisions and that the 'clients' (not a word favoured by many churches), are just there to 'receive from their bounty'. This kind of relationship can easily become patronizing. It may be, initially, that people are so much in need that this is the most appropriate style of working. As soon as possible, however, clients should make choices about activities and services and, as appropriate, be drawn into the decision-making process. If clients have skills they can be encouraged to share them, making them feel valued and perhaps contributing to their being able to integrate more into society.

While it is important that clients do not become dependent upon the service, it is particularly important that they do not become too dependent on certain individual workers. So, for example, if that particular worker is not present it could create anxiety. Similarly, if clients rely too heavily on money or food handouts it may prevent them seeking their own resources. There is another tricky issue. Many must have wondered whether or not to give money to beggars. They must be in need to beg. On the other hand, is this feeding a drug habit? Who are you to decide what is best for them? A parallel problem faces community projects. They have to ask, for example, if clients can come into their premises to shoot or to deal in drugs. Many projects have rules that are made clear to clients, such as no drugs or alcohol on the premises. Some organizations, such as the Samaritans, have rules that volunteers are not to give money. They can give their time or cups of tea and biscuits. In a way, this kind of clarity can be quite a relief for volunteers and other workers. It is important that help centres such as Social Services and night shelters that can and have the expertise and resources to help, are known and the information passed on. There are other dangers in offering help. One church organization arranged with a local café to give a meal to anyone coming with a voucher, which was later paid for by the church. Word soon got round, and in an amazingly short time, the money was used up and the project had to stop. Some community organizations provide and cook meals themselves for clients. Charging a very small, nominal amount for the food can encourage independency and responsibility in those who are on minimal benefits, and can be valued by others too proud to accept handouts. But arrangements are needed for those who really cannot afford anything. Rules are also important to provide for the safety of workers. Clients, unless it is necessary for the functioning of the service, should not be given the address of workers. This is primarily to enable the worker to walk away from their work and not take it home. But it also prevents the client from pestering the worker and even committing violence against him or her. Such boundaries are important.

Management committees

The management committee, too, is a significant part of the leadership of a project. Churches setting up pieces of work, if they are fairly small, often give no thought to management structures. Indeed, the church may consider that their existing structures, such as that of the church parish council or elders' and deacons' meetings is sufficient. But in any substantial project, and certainly if it requires the employment of a worker or workers, then a separate management committee is essential. Indeed, if the project is seeking funds, then it is almost certain that any funding body would expect a management committee to be in place. Much helpful information about the functions and setting up of a management committee and its legal obligations can be found in the literature. Here it is only possible to list some of the key points.

Every organization needs a governing body. If it does not have one, then all the members will legally be considered to be that body. An elected or appointed committee may be given a variety of titles, but its members are considered in law to be acting as agents for the organization. Such a body is usually elected and is required to submit an annual report and audited finances. If the governing body has a formal constitution, which is helpful, then the constitution will state how members are elected, but if it is set up as a trust, then the trust deed will set this out. If the organization is charitable (and this is likely to apply to most church-related community projects), then under charity law, the members of the governing body are the charity trustees. If the organization is registered as a company limited by guarantee, the members of the governing body are the company directors, even if the committee is not called the Board of Directors. An organization which is both a company and a charity is called a charitable company and has only one governing body.

Management committees are there to ensure that the goals of the organization or project are met and to ensure that the project is accountable to the members and/or funders. They are also there to draw on the members' expertise. Sometimes workers in a project can view the management committee as a nuisance, especially if it is perceived that the management committee does not understand the work. Nevertheless, management committees and project workers are there to work in partnership. It is certainly important for the key workers to be present at meetings of the committee. Although the actual responsibility for the project rests with the committee, the day-to-day work is usually delegated to one or more persons, so communication between the two groups is vital. It is not helpful if management-committee members see it as their task directly to exercise authority over the project unless there has been a major crisis and a complete breakdown of relationships.

The primary tasks of the management committee are to create vision, to keep in mind the long-term goals of the organization and to make strategic decisions about the work. The committee is also there to have a concern for the workers and, therefore, to be a key support mechanism in the project. They are there, too, for the clients and to make sure that there are adequate resources (of people, premises and money) to meet their needs. The committee is there to monitor work and to take action when work has not been carried out satisfactorily. A good committee will always consult the users, managers, members of staff and volunteers before making decisions that affect the project. The management committee also has the task of taking legal responsibility for the community project and its actions or inactions. *If the project gets into legal or financial trouble, the members of the management committee may be held to be personally liable.* This requirement can put some people off becoming members of the managing committee, but it is there to make sure that the management committee take their responsibilities seriously. Many organizations take out insurance, and certainly seek advice to make sure that members are not prosecuted. A good management committee provides a very useful support to the leadership of a community project. Working together can provide much more fruitful vision and support than could be ever achieved alone.

Part III

COMMUNITY WORK AND THE COMMUNITY OF FAITH

9

Spirituality in community participation

Popular spirituality

Spirituality is in! In any bookstore a considerable section will range from mysticism to the occult, from psychological self-exploration to New Age and arcane religions. Alternative therapies abound. There is a fascination with ritual and meditation. It has become part of the public realm. The 'spiritual' dimension is deemed important in our education system and in nursing.

Not surprisingly this is a complex and confusing scene, yet one with which it is necessary to come to terms. Josie had a fascinating experience after youth club one evening. A group of the older youngsters, who had been helping, stayed behind for a cup of cocoa. The conversation drifted towards belief in God and questions of spirituality. Josie was asked if she believed in God and why she went to church. She tried to explain how this gave her a point of reference in life and helped her to make sense of it all. In this she was supported by Sandy. Chris and Tricia saw no need for any such 'props' and dismissed faith as an illusion. But Simon and Patsy took another tack. They suggested there is another dimension that impinges on people. Why, they asked, was Tricia wearing a talisman and an armband? Did this not, despite her protests, point to some sort of belief? Simon further declared that the music he so much enjoyed put him in touch with his 'spiritual side'. And what about all those therapies that seem to reach parts that conventional medicine cannot reach? Patsy was more diffident but knew people who went in for meditation and group therapy and it seemed to work for them. Neither Patsy nor Simon saw any need for churchgoing. If God, or whatever this mystery is, is there, one encounters it inwardly and personally, something to do with the feelings. Patsy was convinced she had her guardian angel. You had to believe in something – otherwise how did you know what to do or what is right? As each went home Josie reflected on what had been a strange but exciting experience. Patsy and Simon represented a whole new social reality that had hardly been present when she was a teenager but that was now daily visible on the street. It was not simply that there was a diversity of religions and cultures. Rather there was a buzz which could only be described as a searching for depth and meaning apart from normal secular perspectives. Agreed it sometimes took on whacky forms but it was nonetheless genuine.

First, perhaps, it is a renewal of that romanticism that has been part of the modern world, when revolting against its mechanistic, materialistic industrialized culture, exemplified in Charlie Chaplin's film *Modern Times.* This has come to the surface from time to time. The classic romantics were poets such as Blake and Wordsworth. Parallel expressions can be found in music and the arts. The appeal is to the affective aspects of life, finding meaning through the emotions whether in tranquillity or turbulence. Reality is to be sought for behind the outward surface and in the depths of being.

Yet, at the same time, there is something particular in what is happening today. Many argue that we are entering an entirely new era, signalling the end of modernity. Thus many are welcoming the end of 'the Enlightenment project' of universal rationalism. This is the time of individualism and fragmentation. There is a new social fluidity, aided and abetted by the power of instant communication and the mass migration of peoples across the globe. Cultural values have gone into a melting pot. In this confusion we each have to make our own way, selecting that which makes sense to us. Hence what has been called 'postmodernism'.

Others, however, have preferred to call this 'high modernity' or the 'second modernity', stressing the clear continuities from the past, which have come to a certain climax. Rationalism taught us to question everything and has eroded any sense of received wisdom, authority or social norms. We have ended up with an ultra-individualism that stresses the virtues of choice and self-determination. So the new spirituality can be seen as both conformism to the atomization of society and a protest against the mass conformism of much modern society, a search for an alternative, drawing on neglected areas of human experience.

Yet in the conversation, while there were some clear affinities between the attitudes of Simon and Patsy and those of Josie and Sandy, each of whom accepted the spiritual, there was another division. Simon and Patsy had sided with Chris and Tricia over against Josie and Sandy in dismissing the value of church. This seemed a bit of a mystery. Why was the Church seen as so irrelevant? Indeed it is fashionable to set religion and spirituality in contrast with one another. Yet, in Britain Christianity has for centuries been the vehicle of spirituality. Many people would still see their spiritual aspirations through Christianity. Over 70 per cent claim, in the national census, to be Christian and seek more often than not a Christian burial.

Such an attitude must arise for several reasons. If the new spirituality is part of the rejection of the traditions and authority of the past, then Christianity is part of that past and, indeed, has sometimes embodied what have become regarded as repressive attitudes. So the Church, with other institutions, appears to be old-fashioned. The rise of pop and youth culture has sidelined many cultural patterns. Ironically, however, scientific and technological advances continue to challenge faith. But this still leaves belief as a personal choice in the marketplace of ideas. In a consumer culture it is a matter of what attracts and works for the individual. This is, therefore, for the Church, a time of uncertainty and transition, which can be painful and disruptive.

Building bridges?

This raises important issues to someone like Josie who, engaged in church-based community work, wants to build bridges across the widening chasm between the church community and the wider community. It was natural, therefore, for her to introduce the topic at her next support-group meeting. This helped clarify what was involved and the kinds of decisions that have to be taken.

The question raised by the conversation that evening with the youngsters was the relationship between what our culture understands as spirituality and the Christian tradition. There is clearly much common ground. Both are seeking to affirm the possibility of finding meaning in existence, whether within or beyond the realities of space and time. Both Christian and modern spirituality are uneasy with the obsessive imperialism of certain forms of science and of a narrow positivistic approach to reality. Both, also, seek a holistic approach to the human person that includes whatever is meant by the soul or spirit as well as the body and mind. Moreover, many of the methods found in therapy and meditation have their parallels in, or have been directly borrowed from, the Christian heritage. Others, however, come from other, sometimes esoteric, traditions. At the same time Christian devotion has also been affected by a similar exchange of influences. All these can provide bridges across which it is possible to communicate and meet.

There are, however, also acute differences. Christian spirituality is centred not on the self but on Christ. It is to find in God in Christ a companion and support, yet one who challenges us and calls us to loving service. Life is to be discovered not in ensuring safety, in saving one's self (Mark 8.35 and parallels), but in following in Christ's way, being a disciple. The paradox of freedom is the paradox of love. Furthermore Christian spirituality is not solitary or simply taking that which seems attractive, but about belonging to a community and accepting all the limitations and frustrations, as well as the joys and strengths of committed loyalty. So Christian spirituality is not just about inward feelings of contentment or nearness, but about setting out on a pilgrimage which includes journeying through the dark and lonely places and finding Christ there as much as in times of radiance and peace, and of accepting the trials as well as the joys of belonging to the human race. It is about carrying and being carried, about receiving and giving. This is a challenge to much contemporary spirituality which so often seems shallow and fragile. Christianity's claim is that it presents a more real, more enduring account of the human reality.

In any dialogue, however, communication goes both ways. We ask questions but also listen to the partners in dialogue. For the Christian, this is important because God can meet us in a thousand ways, some very unexpected. The challenge that meets us from our contemporaries' seeking can well remind us of aspects of our own faith that have been neglected and that need to be rediscovered. Or it may be that we have been working on too narrow a canvas and need to look for new ways whereby the Spirit of God comes to us in daily life. We hear the voices of those, often oppressed and suppressed, that open up other dimensions of human experience and ways of living in communal responsibility. The Christian tradition has always pointed to the presence of God beyond the boundaries of faith (John 1.1–14). The old runic Irish proverb reminds us of being blessed by the stranger.

> I met a stranger yester e'en.
> I put food in the eating place,
> Drink into the drinking place.
> Music in the listening place.
> And in the name of the Triune
> He blessed myself and my house,
> My cattle and my dear ones.
> And the lark sang in his song:
> Often, often, often
> Comes the Christ in the stranger's guise.
> Often, often, often
> Comes the Christ in the stranger's guise.
> (Hinton 1984, p. 68)

This is also the theme of the many Russian stories of visitors looked for but not recognized. On the sailing of the Pilgrim Fathers, the Puritan John Robinson declared: 'The Lord hath yet more light and truth to break forth from his holy word.' It is often the one who is thought furthest away who is found to have spoken the truth in love (Ephesians 4.15).

Yet that does not mean that everything has to be accepted. It is a dialogue and we are trying to be true to what we have learnt of God and life in Christ. It is important to 'discern the spirits'

(1 John 4.1). We are not being asked to be naive or irrational but open and venturesome. As in any cross-cultural or inter-faith situation the key ingredients are patience, respect and integrity. And the traffic also goes the other way. Others need to hear what we, in humility, have found to be true in Christ. If that is not spoken then we have not been true to ourselves and they are the poorer. There may be occasion for set-piece discussions and dialogue; but mainly it is through working together, being part of the same scene, in daily encounter, where knowledge and trust can grow. This then bubbles up into the kind of conversation Josie had that evening.

Elements of Christian spirituality

Josie and her support group found that they wanted to take the issue of spirituality further. All too often there is little reflection or even understanding of the nature and possibilities of Christian spirituality. The public Christian festivals, such as Christmas and Easter, have been so overlaid, is there any real awareness of their central Christian meaning? Even at the more routine levels of regular practice there is little sense of discipline and a somewhat attenuated practice. By and large, in the post-Christian secular society in which we live, many corporate customs have been lost and there is little memory of what it means to belong to a faith.

What then are the marks and qualities of Christian spirituality? Basically it is the form and expression of one's relationship with God. It tends, therefore, principally to be about prayer and worship but it is wider than that, since one's spiritual life creates the context for and gives meaning to the whole life of discipleship. It has two dimensions: the inner life of a personal relationship with God and, in Christ, the neighbour; and the outward expression of that life in personal and shared acts of worship and devotion. This latter incorporates an element of discipline, though disciplines can, of course, become routine and perhaps a formality. Even so, inner habit and deep relationships are also forged out of commitment and regularity as well as from innovation and surprise. Moreover it is important in a busy and stressful life to ensure that the essential, deep dimensions are not forgotten or allowed to drift from memory. God may not forget us but it is easy to forget God.

The first thing to note is the rich and amazing variety. There is an almost infinite mine from which can be quarried words and styles and practices, both new and old. A glimpse at a standard hymn book gives some small idea of the debt owed. Each generation has found ways of meeting with God and expressing their adoration and indebtedness as well as finding the path to the intimate place of solemn or ecstatic presence. In recent times there have been signs of renewal in prayer and worship stimulated both by the increase of ecumenical freedom and the revivalist charismatic movements, further enriched by insights and practices from other religious traditions and even secular sources.

A second discovery is the necessity for each person to work out their own spiritual practice. It may be true that earlier generations were provided with frameworks that offered support and a yardstick for acceptable behaviour; but even in those days it was still a personal journey. Today, in a more open market, it is a matter of finding one's personal way to respond to the tradition. At the heart of Christian spirituality is the Eucharist (see Chapter 11), but even here there is a surprising breadth of practice and understanding. There are also, of course, tried and recognized patterns of spiritual discipline and prayer but these are there to support and help, not to become a chain. Where one finds foundations and enrichment is the result of many factors. We are all on a spiritual journey and at different stages. We are all temperamentally different and what suits one will not suit another. We are all in different contexts, under different constraints, needing to express different needs and hopes, joys and fears. The repositories of wisdom and the opportunities to explore both serve the desire to live within the love and will of God who has called us to be with Christ in the world. So an important aim of the support group was to help Josie work on these issues that confronted her, something to which she had to return every so often as the work changed around her and she changed with it.

Third, the Christian life is always lived as a member of the People of God. This in practice means belonging to a particular congregation. It is through participation in the worship of the particular place that one is brought into the universal fellowship of the Church. There is a question here for the church-related community worker. How far, as a community worker, is it necessary to be identified with the congregation on which the work is based? There are clear advantages and disadvantages in both directions. Josie is glad she is a member of the congregation that is employing her. This makes her clearly part of the leadership team. It brings her into the worshipping and social life of the congregation. She is known to those members of the church who would not otherwise meet her from one weekend to the next. She is embedded in the wider community both as a community worker and as a member of the church. The difficulty is living on the job. Not only is she on call for longer but she finds it difficult to draw the boundaries between her job and participation in the church's life as an ordinary member. This, though, she shares with any minister in pastoral charge.

Josie often talks about this with Elsie, with whom she trained, but who does not live on the patch on which she works. To separate the two, argues Elsie, allows her to have a clear space between her home life and what is a demanding and stressful job. It also means that she is 'off duty' when in the worship and fellowship of the church, thereby more easily refreshing her heart and mind. It allows her, in the church, to exercise skills and interests different from those used for her job. Her place of work becomes just that in relation to the members of that church. Role definitions are very clear. The disadvantage is that she is not so readily part of the community around the community centre. She is a commuter, more like the social worker or teacher. While a community worker will have a preference it will largely be circumstances that will dictate which style to adopt. It is, however, a matter that should figure in the discussion of any appointment.

Of central importance, both Josie and Elsie agreed, is to determine the broad structure of the pattern of one's spiritual discipline. First is how a regular structure for prayer and reflection is to be built into the work pattern. Elsie finds that she can call in at the cathedral on the way either to or from work where she can sit quietly. Josie, however, uses the weekly team meeting, which always includes a longish period of silence. It also provides a regular time with the Scriptures as along with the team she wrestles with the chosen passage from the lectionary. Elsie, on the other hand, has a daily set of readings and a monthly Bible study in her house group. This is supplemented by other theological reading to complement the necessary professional reading that the job enjoins. Josie belongs to a reading group that meets once a term to discuss a chosen volume. Elsie is more haphazard but would expect to read at least one substantial book a year, normally in the summer period.

There is also a wider context. As part of her contract Elsie is given time for personal (not professional, which is another clause) study and/or development. This she uses variously for reading time or to take in a theological conference or to go on retreat or to go to an event such as Spring Harvest or to visit Taizé. Josie, however, is a member of the Iona Community which has a structured framework of gatherings throughout the year. There are numerous other orders and societies that can similarly provide support and opportunities to refresh the heart and mind.

Theological reflection

One of the problems in Christian spirituality is to link together the all too solid reality of work and the inner life of faith. This arises primarily for two reasons. First, there is in our society a wedge driven between the interior and personal world of the spirit and the public, secular world of society. Making connections that allows faith to inform practice is never easy. The second is that all of us need to grow further into God. There is a gap between the depths of Christian sanctity and our appropriation of grace. These three have to be drawn together: the demands of the world, the riches of faith and our own pilgrimage. This is the task of theological reflection. Nor is it easy. Indeed it is probably the hardest dimension of discipleship.

In recent years much attention has been given to this concern and patterns and models have been devised to enable people to develop skills. Here is not the place to discuss these in detail (see bibliography). It is right, however, to underline the importance of this both as part of training and as a regular part of practice and personal evaluation. It is, as we have seen, also a key part of the pastoral cycle (Chapter 4). Practice in theological reflection, corporately and personally, enables the gospel perspective to become engrained in us, so that we have a resource instinctively to hand in the day-to-day affairs when there is not usually room for deliberate reflection.

An exercise of theological reflection will be an act of prayer. Whether it is about a specific incident or a particular person, a broad issue or a policy decision, it is important to set the act of reflection within the perspective of the Kingdom of God, which includes ourselves, those about whom we are concerned, the whole socio-economic context as well as the hope for and yearning after wisdom, justice and peace.

There will, of course, be considered and concerned attention to the social realities involved in this exercise, both in its particularity of time and place and how it is illuminated by the insights of sociology, psychology, economics and the other human sciences.

Equally it is necessary to struggle with the theological resources to hand. This is more than snatching at an uninformed and ill-digested mishmash of theological themes or texts. Theological reflection asks what lies within and behind the wisdom of Scripture and doctrine. How do they witness to and give insights into the creative, redeeming and sustaining love of God? What does it mean to be caught up in the dynamic of living in a reality that is shaped by such perspectives? How can we discern the lure of the Kingdom in the time of the not yet (Matthew 13.24–30)? Theological reflection is a craft or an art, honed by long practice, not a technique or a set of rules for finding out best answers to a question. It is about so indwelling both the world and God that the two are seen together and not as contrasted spheres of existence. The one is not present without the other. This, as Bonhoeffer (1955) argues, is the point of the incarnation. The two spheres, to use his terminology, become one in Christ. Therefore for the Christian they are never apart. This is the basis of

Christian ethics; learning to see the reality of the world through the reality of God.

> There are not two realities, but only one reality, and that the reality of God, which has become manifest in Christ in the reality of the world. Sharing in Christ we stand at once in both the reality of God and the reality of the world. The reality of Christ comprises the reality of the world.
> (Bonhoeffer 1955, pp. 63–4)

An art or a craft, however, is all about imagination, so as to see within, through and under the presenting symptoms to what is actual and fundamental and true. This is not a quixotic process or a matter of personal whim. It is shaped by, but also released through, the insights of faith found in and through the experience of the grace of God in our lives, in the lives of those around us and the saints down the years and across the globe. Nor does it ignore the harsh reality of human existence. It seeks to find in it where the burden of sin is carried and the signs of the Kingdom are beginning to appear. In the end the craft-worker or artist, through learning, discipline and practice, begins to work by a kind of intuition through the trained eye and hand. This is what, in a professional context, Donald Schön (1955) called the 'reflective practitioner' and Edward Farley (1980), in a more theological setting, called 'habitus' and Aristotle called 'virtue', or orientation of the soul towards the true, the good and the beautiful. But this can never be taken for granted. As professionals have always to keep abreast of their knowledge and skills, so the theological practitioner is always in need of renewal.

So Christian spirituality is to be at that place where Jesus is found and to see the world and ourselves through his eyes. To borrow from Rowan Williams, 'We stand where Jesus stands as Christian believers, and pray as Jesus prays; and in standing in that place before God as "Abba", we share equally in Jesus' directedness towards the good and the healing of the world' (Waller and Ward 1992, p. 2).

Again we can return to Bonhoeffer (1955). We are, he says, to be conformed to Christ who is 'the Incarnate, Crucified and Risen One' (p. 18). This, first, places us precisely at that point in space and time where we have therefore been given our reality and where, in God, we find Christ. So we stand with Christ in the midst. Second, however, Christ is also the Crucified One, the one who is marginalized and broken in a world that is dangerous and destructive and deceitful. In both our strengths and our weaknesses we are part of the crucifying world. Yet at the same time we suffer with the crucified Lord on behalf of the world, bearing its pain and estrangement, wounded by its arrogance and wilfulness. For us, as for Christ, this is only possible as we find support in and from the Father. This, however, is not the last word, for the Crucified One is also the Risen One, the Lord who, in and through the cross, brings new life and hope, turns tears to laughter and emerges from darkness into light. This is not only promise but part of being with Christ in the world, for in the shadow and fear there is also newness, sacrificial love, persistent hope and unexpected beauty. Here, too, we are in the presence of God who has, in Christ, 'gathered together things heavenly and earthly'. All we are called to do is to find it true and to witness to the presence of Christ in our place where he stands with us.

The living reality

What then does all this mean? Josie and Elsie sometimes share how they find themselves coping in their stressful work and what faith is for them.

Five things stand out. First, the reality of prayer. This refers not to the inspiration in worship, nor to personal meditations, valuable as they are, nor to stories of wonderfully answered prayer, though they do not doubt that there have been times when circumstances reflected the yearnings of the heart. Rather it is the recognition of the continual presence of God and that at any time one can share a concern, an encounter, a sudden crisis with God. As Elsie said, 'It is possible just to chuck the situation at God and know that that was OK; after all God has stuck us here, so it is God's responsibility in the end, not mine.' Fear becomes manageable with a nod to God who is there too. Or when anger overwhelms at the sight of cruelty, the crucified

Lord is also remembered and there is also hope and some small openness to the oppressor as well as the victim. Anything is material for prayer. It is Brother Lawrence who is remembered for his discovery of the possibility of prayer in the loneliness and humdrum routine of a kitchen.

Second, it is easier to accept the burden and not be crushed. In community work, as in some other professions, there is an engagement with people that can become more than we can bear. This is about empathy and detachment (Chapter 9). But for the Christian, standing with Christ in the midst of the world, there is a calling to suffering service. Those around cannot be reduced to cases. Yet it is necessary to accept that there is only so much that can be done and beyond that the responsibility is not ours. This is not to leave it to fate or luck but to find that the burden-bearing Lord is there before, with and after our best efforts. Fortunately, too, there are visible rewards, like the time a bright young man stopped Josie in the street. 'Remember me? I was the one you consoled when my brother died of drugs and my mother deserted me. I will never forget what you did.' Often, however, it is a matter of hoping that it is all worth it and whether one has even made a dent. Charles Elliott is helpful here. Addressing the immensity of world poverty and the Christian calling to serve the Kingdom, he suggests:

> It is when we acknowledge ourselves as power*less* – as caught, trapped, unable to achieve any improvement in either our own inner lives or in the external forces to which they give rise – it is then we become penetrable by the Spirit of God. As long as we imagine that the world can be changed by our activities, our good works, our energy, we substitute our effort for the power of God. That is as ineffective as it is blasphemous. 'For thine is the Kingdom, and the power . . .' we pray, incidentally making a revealing and overlooked juxtaposition – and then, all too frequently, behave as if his is the Kingdom and ours its power – and glory too. (Elliott 1985, p. 19)

This is not an appeal to quietism. Elliott was a one-time Director of Christian Aid. It is to know that we are ourselves part of the weight that is on Christ's shoulders as well as being a living, serving witness.

Third, both spoke of what can only be described as their 'reverse conversion'. Like Peter in the encounter with Cornelius, they had discovered that while they had thought they were there to serve the needs of those around, it was they who were being enriched. God's goodness, peace, justice and beauty were to be found in unexpected places. Peter had to admit that Cornelius, the Roman centurion, an officer in the occupying forces, was God's word to him (Acts 11.1–18). They found that community work is as much about receiving as giving and finding gospel realities which they had to learn, in the lives of those who apparently were far from the Kingdom. They pointed to fierce sacrificial love in many single teenage mothers, the compassion of the mugged old lady for the teenage druggy, the seemingly boundless hope of people fighting a clearly ill-conceived re-housing scheme, or the bravery of those willing to resist the yobs and bring some sense of local pride. Here, for those who wish to see, are the signs of the Kingdom, embedded in the lives of ordinary people almost overwhelmed by dreariness and disappointment. Old familiar spiritual realities are given new meaning and depth. Faith becomes trust where there has been little or no experience of trust. Hope becomes never giving up even in the face of constant frustration. Love is about acceptance and kindness for those that have little to attract us (see Mary McAleese in Ballard, 1990). Through paying attention, Josie and Elsie find a fresh vision of Christ's presence and, for themselves, a new sense of proportion, accepting the grace of ministry from those who would be surprised and even shocked if they were to be told that is what they are doing. Here the words of Margaret Walsh, a Catholic sister living in community on a deprived housing estate, ring true: 'Because I have been evangelised by these people myself, I am convinced that by listening to them, learning from them and being creative in our response to meet their needs, the whole Church could be renewed' (Sedgwick 1995, p. 67).

For community workers, however, spirituality and theological reflection is about creating and sustaining community. This is most clearly seen in the experience of the Ecclesial Base Communities of Latin America and similar groups elsewhere. Here Scripture and experience are welded together in an hermeneutic encounter that creates the prophetic and pastoral dynamic for action. Stories are numerous as to how, for example, the parables of Jesus illuminate and energize the struggle for land reform or economic self-sufficiency. It is not often that opportunities arise in this country which are comparable to such situations. The groups we are working with seldom meet in the context of worship, Bibles to hand. Rather the process works in reverse. The establishment of a group around a particular need or aim engenders not only a sense of purpose but also a web of relationships that both contribute to the task and have real spin-off effects. Friendships are made, cares and anxieties shared, skills transferred, support given at times of difficulty, fresh levels of responsibility accepted and a sense of worth discovered. Alongside the commitment to the task there can be celebrations, and the mundane routines are lubricated with tea. In unspoken ways there is a quality that could only be called spiritual, even eucharistic. Hints, sometimes from surprising quarters, tell us that others find this too, though without the words to express what they are feeling. Occasionally it is possible to bring this to the surface. Elsie recalled community weddings, ostensibly secular with perhaps a touch of religion, when ritual tipped over into a desire to offer thanks, and wishing luck was more like prayer. Again, there were funerals, crowded with neighbours and workmates as well as family and friends, which touched the borders of heaven as farewell was said to the deceased. Familiar words again took on meaning. On other occasions a moving or defining moment is celebrated with a poem and a candle, or with silence and shared comments. Perhaps things have gone full circle, for we are back here at that point where folk spirituality and Christian faith meet. The Christian will both affirm and rejoice in the discovery and gently witness to the ultimate source of fulfilment in God as found in Jesus.

This leads, fifth, to a further point. The community worker, like the minister, doctor, or social worker, is usually a stranger from outside, with skills, authority and resources. They act as a necessary catalyst, needed to kick-start a reaction towards community formation. This is indeed a gift to be offered without shame. But there is a tension here. Community work moves from the bottom up. How far can the community worker really identify with the local community; indeed, ought they? How can we become sharers in the reality we serve and yet be signs of hope and sources of strength so that others can begin to find hope and strength?

The Church has widely recognized 'Christ's preferential option for the poor', 'friend of tax collectors and sinners'. This identification allowed him to be dismissed by those in authority as just a country bumpkin, a wanderer from Galilee of the Gentiles, with no formal qualifications. He carried no authority other than his innate personality. Yet for those who heard and responded, Jesus was, through various levels of understanding, the Messiah, or at least a prophet. Here is the authority of the servant, servant of God whose service was to bring life into the world. It is not easy to accept this anonymity of authority, whether of position or skills or commission. This, too, is well caught by Margaret Walsh.

> Attempting to do things for people tends not to be life giving in the long run and perhaps is often a reflection of our own misguided need and our inborn tendency to dominate and so to treat people as objects of our charity. Only by walking alongside others and being with them, can we grow into the type of community that Christ envisioned for his Kingdom. (Sedgwick 1995, p. 57)

Perhaps that sums up the spirituality appropriate for a community worker. Josie and Elsie recognized the challenge. None, surely, will claim to have arrived. The joy is that, to some degree, we are on the way and that, in and through Christ, it is possible both to serve, even in our weakness, and to be supported in the stumbling progress towards the fullness of God.

10

Worship in and for the community

Worship is the heart of the life of the Church. Through its worship it expresses its faith and hope and love and offers praise and thanksgiving to God in Christ. Through worship it is shaped and renewed so that it may be conformed to the life and pattern of Christ. This is, in almost all Christian traditions, manifest most clearly in and through the Eucharist. Here is laid out the story of redemption into which the Church is drawn and by which the Church, in its corporate existence and in its members, lives.

So this chapter asks three questions. How do we express our commitment in and for the community in the worship of the congregation? How can and does our worship express and build up the community life and fellowship of the congregation? What are some of the ways by which those, on the edges of the Church or enquiring into faith or even in the wider community, can find meaning and even the possibility of prayer in and through their contact with the Church?

'For all nations'?

In the cleansing of the temple, as Mark tells it:

> [Jesus] entered the temple and began to drive out those who were selling and those who were buying in the temple, and he overturned the tables of the money-changers and the seats of those who sold doves; and he would not allow anyone to carry anything through the temple. He was teaching, and saying, 'Is it not written, "My house shall be called a house of prayer for all the nations"? But you have made it a den of robbers.' (Mark 11.15–19)

Something was clearly radically wrong to give rise to so much indignation. The clue is to be found in Jesus' words, which echo Isaiah 56.7 and Jeremiah 7.11. Jesus was not attacking the trade in the sacred space, though doubtless some were able and willing to corrupt the system. He was attacking the way that it represented a spirit of exclusivity – the need to prevent the outside world contaminating the holy place by insisting on the approved sacrificial animals and currency. The reference in Jeremiah is not to robbery but to the need for bandits to have a stronghold from which they can defy their pursuers. But, as Isaiah said, the temple is 'for all nations', offering a welcome to all humankind. It was this that Jesus looked for in vain. It was this that Mark symbolically underlined when the curtain of secrecy was ripped in two at the hour of Christ's death (Mark 15.38). Thus, too, the new Jerusalem will be an open city into which all the nations can bring their riches and bathe in the light of the glory of God and from which shall flow living water that washes and cleanses the whole of creation (Revelation 21.22–23).

This is what Christian worship should emulate: all nations coming to the altar and the source of the cleansing power of God's Spirit reaching out into every corner of life. Desmond Tutu tells movingly of his experience as Dean of Johannesburg,

> . . . watching a multi-racial crowd file up to the altar rails to be communicated, the one bread and the one cup given by a mixed team of clergy and lay ministers, with a multi-racial choir, servers and sidesmen – and all this in apartheid mad South Africa – then tears sometimes streamed down my cheeks, tears of joy that it could be that indeed Jesus Christ had broken down the wall of partition and here were the first fruits of the eschatological community right in front of my eyes, enacting the message in several languages on the notice board outside that this is the house of prayer for peoples of all races who are welcome at all times. (Tutu 1983, p. 135)

But all too often, perhaps unwittingly and almost certainly not deliberately, the people of God are anxious – about their identity, about God's promises, about survival – and preoccupied with our own needs or hurts or security. Perhaps, even, we think that God owes us a reward for our faithfulness. So the constant task is to ensure that the voice of Jesus is heard, even at the deepest and most sacred space of our own particular world. 'Strive first for the kingdom of God and his righteousness, and all these things will be given to you as well' (Matthew 6.33). He directs our attention away from ourselves to God and the world where the Kingdom seeks to be established. This is the priestly calling of the Church, to stand before God with the world, offering praise and prayer, and in the world as witnesses to God's mercy and grace.

Surveying the scene

The churches of Winkelthorpe, to mark a new covenant of shared witness and mission, decided to undertake a major study of what was happening to the town and how the various congregations could respond better together and severally. Liz, the Anglican non-stipendiary assistant priest, was convenor of the group on prayer and worship, chosen because she had done a special study of liturgy as part of her training. The Catholic member was Joan, a health professional, the Methodist was Ena, a teacher, and the Baptist was Ben, their youth worker. They were a pretty eclectic bunch and they wondered how they would get on from their very different traditions, but afterwards they agreed that they had learnt a lot and been drawn closer together.

They set themselves a threefold initial task: to visit several churches in the region where interesting work was being done, to do some reading about worship and mission, becoming better acquainted with their own tradition as well as following up other leads, and, then, to talk about their own congregations, noting their strengths and weaknesses of their worship in relation to community concerns. Three somewhat surprising conclusions came out of this process.

The first was how greatly each denomination had been influenced, often unwittingly, by recent movements within the churches, which meant that nowadays, prayers, music and ways of doing worship were often very familiar whichever church one was in. The earliest was the Liturgical Movement, at its height in the fifties and sixties, which lies behind the pattern of much contemporary liturgy, informing most of the worship manuals and prayer books since then. Its characteristic mark was the rediscovery of the Eucharist as the central act of worship of the People of God, who gather in fellowship, expressing their common life in and for the world in the service of God. Somewhat later, in the eighties and nineties, the Charismatic Movement, while it emphasized freedom in the Spirit and personal experiential faith, also laid great stress on the shared participation, expressed through song and event. Then, third, liberation theology, emanating from Latin America, stressed the radical social and economic nature of the gospel. Characteristically it worked out of small community groups gathered round the mass and the Bible which explored 'God's option for the poor'. In the West its influence was felt in concern for the inner city and the marginalized in society. It has also affected worship and spirituality through the work of such groups as Christian Aid and the Iona Community.

The second discovery was that, despite the differences in the styles of worship, there was a fundamental 'gospel logic' at work, for worship corresponds to the gracious relationship between God and the world. This was not surprising for those most directly affected by the Liturgical Movement, but even the Baptists could be seen to be working to the same imperatives. For all, communion, if not a weekly service, was clearly regarded as the normative expression of Christian worship. This, broadly, consists of five moments: the Gathering, which for the Baptists tended to be an extended period of worship and praise and song; the Word, with Scripture and preaching or reflective sharing, listening to God; the Response, through offering and intercession; the Breaking of the Bread or Act of Communion, where the fellowship in Christ is actualized; and the Dismissal, when the fellowship and each disciple is sent out for their particular service in the world.

Third, they redefined for themselves the extempore in worship. Familiarly 'extempore' has been assumed to mean 'made up on the spot, without a script', contrasted with the use of a set text from a prayer book. There is certainly a place for spontaneous worship and freedom of expression, most usually in small groups though also in congregational worship. But there is another and more important meaning to the phrase, which is 'out of and in response to the needs of the present situation'. It is this that should inform the People of God in their responsibility to the world, whether spontaneously or in prepared ways, whether the words are our own or borrowed from others because they say well what we want to say. So Christian worship has both a given theological and traditional content and yet is particular to each and every time and place; it is both expressed in time-honoured ways and is open to the surprise of the Spirit.

These considerations led on to the three questions about how their worship could better express their own commitment to being part of their town's community and their service in and for it.

Praying as a community of faith

The framework for tackling the first question, on how the Christian community can express its concern for the world in its worship, was provided by the most recent rite of the Church of England, *Common Worship*. The others found that they could easily apply it to their own situations.

The first point was the amount of shared words. The congregation is active and participatory and not an audience. This is an expression of its corporate nature, which is itself part of the meaning of being human. This is facilitated if the service, or at least the places where there is congregational participation, is accessible for each worshipper, in print or some form of projection. Familiar words are learnt by heart, a repertoire that can be extended if carefully introduced. By careful strategies it was possible to have both the familiar and the innovative working together.

The offertory includes both the money collected and the bread and wine. One of the emphases of the Liturgical Movement seems to have been largely lost here. In the Catholic Mass, and in some of the other communion services, these words, or a variant on them, are used as the bread and wine are brought to the table:

> Blessed are you, Lord God of all creation; through your goodness we have this bread (wine) to set before you, which earth has given and human hands have made.

This is a reminder that we are making an offering not only of the natural gifts but of our daily labour. In the Orthodox tradition each communicant places a small loaf in the basket at the door along with their monetary gift. While these are now prepared, it was presumably originally brought from the family kitchen. Increasingly, too, the bread used is an ordinary loaf, bought from the bakery or made as part of someone's weekly cooking. The wine (or red grape juice) similarly comes off the supermarket shelves. In these elements are found all the commerce and the toil of our globalized world. Similarly the money that is placed on the plates is not simply a way of paying for the church but is also the dedication of one's life and possessions. So the offertory procession, in which the bread and wine and the money offering should be combined, is that point in the service, as part of our response to the gospel, when we offer ourselves and are laid on the altar. Our lives, in all their ambiguity, are handed over to God to be transformed and made part of the service of the Kingdom. This is continued by our giving of time, talents and substance in the service of the wider community, locally, nationally and internationally. All wealth is for service and the poor and needy have a first call on our care.

The offered gifts are received. God takes us and welcomes us. We are embraced back into the household. This is what is meant by confession. Tired and weak, the wavering and the doubters, the strong and those who overestimate their strength, those who are caught up in the pressures and demands of the world, often finding themselves in places of compromise and ambiguity – these are the ones that come to prayer. Sin has been dumbed down in common understanding in our society to those deeds of wrongdoing that we seldom recognize in ourselves. Rather, sin is to be part, personally and corporately, of society, where mud sticks, corners are cut, tempers fray, winning is all, victors gloat and responsibilities are evaded. We are part of society and all its ills. Moreover, with a stronger doctrine of sin there comes an even stronger doctrine of grace, because God refuses to let the world or us go and offers loving care in and through the very stuff of life, despite its brokenness. However, in a highly individualized culture this idea of belonging together is unpalatable. Such an insight can only be built up over time, through teaching, explanation and the use of good words. It is interesting that the Iona Community has reintroduced the Celtic practice of mutual absolution – first the congregation confesses and is absolved and then the celebrant is absolved by the congregation – which catches the idea of our sharing together in sin and forgiveness. In the Catholic mass, confession is a corporate sharing of confession and absolution. An increasing number of other sources also offer suitable words that can be used both in confession and at other points in the service that express the complex web that is our sinful world.

Many congregations now actively pass the peace. This, which is one of the precious gifts of grace (Galatians 5.22), represents our acceptance of and being accepted by the company of God's people. It is a potent enacting of community bonding. On occasion it can almost become an event, as when members of the congregation greet each other at Christmas. Where better to wish each other a happy Christmas, even though it takes a quarter of an hour? But, week by week, the peace is the liturgical expression of welcome that is offered at the start and finish of service at the door, in the coffee lounge, at the fellowship meal and through the whole life of the fellowship, and this welcome should spill out into the world around bringing healing and reconciliation.

This was a theme that was returned to on a number of occasions. Even in a small town where it can be usual to meet neighbours while out shopping and down the street, it is still true that people are often comparative strangers. It is even more true in cosmopolitan urban centres. Even in congregations that pride themselves on a high level of personal fellowship it can be admitted that little is known of the weekday world that members inhabit. How can the bond of fellowship be sustained if there is little interest in the domestic and work-time circumstances of fellow Christians? News bulletins, it was suggested, should include items other than births and illness. It is good to hear stories about people's hopes and joys and anxieties in family and work. To know that someone you know is part of a situation that is current news (a hospital closure, a development plan, or promotion) is to experience it more directly and realistically and to be able to pray for each other in an informed way.

The eucharistic drama brings us to the heart of the gospel. Here the bread and wine become both the vehicle and the symbols of the story which is our story; or better, our story, given to God, is transfigured into God's story, which is the death and resurrection of Christ. The bread is broken and we are crucified with Christ for the redemption of the world. The bread is shared, which is both a communion, a coming together in the one body, and a strengthening for the task. 'Give us,' we pray, 'our daily bread'; which could be translated 'our marching rations', food for the journey. This leads to the dismissal which today, familiarly, includes the injunction 'to love and serve the Lord'. So there is a strengthening and a transformation. We become the Body of Christ, the bread of heaven, in order to feed the world.

There were other suggestions. There is value in using different media, from the visual to the dramatic. Another was to use the Christian year more creatively. The great festivals are Christ-centred, but even here there is opportunity to root the story more clearly into the contemporary world of present-day Jerusalem and Bethlehem, which are also parables of our humanity. There are, however, other commemorations. All Saints tide allows us to remember our own story and to rediscover ourselves as part of the whole Church of God. Harvest points most clearly both to 'the fruit of the earth' and to 'the work of human hands', when we are most conscious of the life of the world around. One World Week, in October, and Christian Aid Week, in May, impel us to widen our horizons globally and also to recognize the world that has come onto our doorstep. At other time there are calls to remember different aspects of life such as education and homelessness, AIDs and refugees and asylum-seekers.

Praying the community

This brought the members of the 'prayer and worship' group to think about their responsibility to the world in worship. One of the great privileges of the Christian life is the priestly ministry of intercession. The writer of 1 Timothy urges:

> First of all then, I urge that supplications, prayers, intercessions, and thanksgivings be made for everyone, for kings and all who are in high positions, so that we may lead a quiet and peaceable life, in all godliness and dignity. This is right and acceptable in the sight of God our Saviour, who desires everyone to be saved and to come to the knowledge of the truth. (1 Timothy 2.1–2, NRSV)

The Church plays its part in the High Priestly ministry of Christ (Hebrews 4.14—5.10). This is the mandate for the daily round of prayer and praise in both the regular hours of corporate prayer in church and monastery and in the secret place of personal prayer of each of Christ's people. In our common worship the intercessions ought to be seen as one of the highlights of the liturgy, when offered before God on behalf of the world.

Here is one of the links between the congregation and the social activity done in its name. To intercede takes seriously the welfare of the community and it also strengthens those who are involved in the various activities. This was confirmed by Ben who, as a church-based youth worker, found it a source of strength to know that his work was being supported in prayer. He also valued being able, in pastorally sensitive ways, to bring the needs of those with whom he worked to the attention of fellow church members, from anxieties over exams or career choices, to someone in trouble or suffering a loss. In a small community news and rumours travel fast. To have facts in the open and setting them in the context of prayer can enable more creative reactions. Moreover, often without saying anything, the youngsters also appreciated it. It shows that the old fuddy-duddies are really interested.

A number of suggestions were made to enhance the place of intercession. There is a traditional use of candles and incense, something widely appreciated outside the Church. Churches have places where intercessions can be gathered – a notice board, a book or a box. These tend to be used for personal needs – those known to the congregation. Encouragement should be given to include matters of import to the neighbourhood or wider. There should also be a regular coverage of people and concerns. One church magazine listed all the members regularly. There are prayer diaries for the Church worldwide, both denominational and broader, and diocesan and district prayer calendars. There are, too, anthologies and authored collections of prayers and worship material from around the world. But there seems to be nothing to provide a framework for regular prayer over one's village, town or city. Perhaps this is something that can only be done locally, taking note of local customs and celebrations.

In these ways it is possible to counter the prevalence of impersonal and vague topics for intercession and to root them in the messiness of actual living. To illustrate this Ben recalled when there had been a strike on at a factory which was a major employer in the area. Inevitably some people in the congregation were involved directly, either as managers, employees or customers. Feelings ran high. How was the minister to frame prayers for such a situation? Was he to be bland, asking for reconciliation in a complex and contentious set of issues, or by indicating what was at stake and being open to being accused of taking sides? What he did was to ask the congregation to examine where each of them stood, and to allow the different attitudes to be voiced so that the divisions were openly manifest. Then he called for prayer, both silent and led, offering up each of the problems and attitudes, asking God to be with all involved and for the Spirit to come alongside (John 14.15–17) in creative ways. Not all were happy, but the majority found that they were better able to understand those with whom they disagreed and felt that they had both prayed more realistically and given the Spirit greater freedom.

Other ways can be found, some more suitable for small informal groups, to bring local concerns before the congregation. The local paper covers local planning, policing, welfare and educational issues, as well as matters of general interest. People are usually willing to talk about themselves, their family and their situation. Here is a resource for understanding not only their personal concerns but also the dilemmas and problems that are part of daily life. Some congregations have undertaken a prayer walk as a public demonstration of concern. Visitors, perhaps distributing leaflets or magazines, can ask those they meet of their concerns and assure people of prayer. It is sometimes surprising how grateful people are. A more low-key approach would be to work on a large map of the area and discuss what and whom they know in different parts of the district. In an act of worship there can be a time of preparation, so that the items for prayer are already in people's minds before the actual praying starts, led by the minister or others who have prepared the intercessions, or even through open discussion.

The mystery of intercession is not to bombard God with demands or even requests but aligning ourselves with the Spirit at work in the world, believing that this is important and effective without asking how or why. It does, however, also make a difference to us. We may find ourselves doing something different in response, from giving to volunteering. Vitally, however, prayer puts things into a wider perspective – the perspective of the Kingdom – and into God' hands.

Praying with the community

Last, the Church offers hospitality and tries to enable those who may have little experience and understanding of worship to be meaningfully engaged. At the normal regular Sunday services strangers will often be present, crossing a threshold into what may be for them a very strange place. Everything should be made as smooth and welcoming as possible. Sometimes a companion in the pew is welcome. There are familiar practices that are taken for granted but that can be awkward for the occasional visitor.

Christmas has become popular with its carols and midnight mass. There is also a string of other services, often for schools and organizations. Here are opportunities for carefully planned and innovative acts of reflection and worship. Christmas also highlights the clash between folk tradition and the faith of the Church. There are other occasions which also lend themselves to being designed with the visitor in mind. In rural areas especially, harvest can be a notable occasion, sometimes being a massive community event where the service sits alongside the feasting and dancing. In a more urban context harvest can relate to local commercial and industrial activities through, for example, Industrial Mission. St Luke's tide, he being the patron saint of medicine, can similarly be used in relation to the health and social care professions; and One World Week allows a window on the world to be opened up and a reminder of the point of fair trade.

More often, however, contact is through the occasional offices – infant baptism or dedication, marriage and funerals. Again every effort can be made to make it a gift to those for whom it is an important family event. As part of our witness in the community these are opportunities to express the Church's interest and pastoral sensitivity, affirming them in the realities of their daily lives. To be ill prepared and insensitive is to send out all the wrong signals.

As part of this pastoral concern, in many places, commemorative services are held from time to time to which people on the appropriate mailing list are invited. That this will happen should be made clear in the initial contact. All Saints/All Souls tide is the natural time to remember the dead; St Valentine's Day, now a major secular festival, a time to celebrate marriage; and Mothering Sunday, another commercial season, a time to bring together those who have been baptized or dedicated as infants. Others have begun to provide 'seekers' services' on a more regular basis with the same object in mind. As the memory of the Church and what it stands for fades in the popular mind such initiatives become the more important as ways of rediscovering Church in a fresh way. They also become increasingly difficult to execute.

There are also those occasions, more frequent in the city or town centre, when the civic authorities or others look for a church service in relation to special occasions, such as the Mayor's inauguration or the Assizes. Remembrance is almost universal. From time to time there can be acts of worship celebrating national and other events. Planning always has to be meticulous, creative and, hopefully, collaborative. These days there is the desire to be inclusive. Interdenominational issues are comparatively easy to deal with; but now there are matters of inter-faith collaboration as well as secularized sensitivities. How these are dealt with will differ and here is not the place to enter into an extended discussion. Whatever the practical solution, there is a tension between the need to be true to the Christian witness and the genuine desire to be open. But that is a tension inherent in the gospel, which declares God's loving kindness to the whole of creation that is revealed in the particularity of incarnation.

There is also the long tradition of taking faith and witness out into the public arena. From the medieval mystery plays and festival processions to the Salvation Army band and carols in the shopping mall, people have gathered round to hear and look, as they have been asked to relate to the deeper reality that is hidden in all the business of the everyday.

Authentic worship springs out of the juxtaposition of the gospel and culture. It is not surprising, therefore, that in an age of rapid social change and growing pluriformity there is a plethora of new, often creative and innovative ways of expressing faith, reflecting the opportunities, hopes and fears of our times. These are often beyond the fringes of the traditional ecclesial structures. For those working with people to enable them to discover their own authentic and communal reality, part of community development is to free people to express themselves and their lives together in worship. What they come up with will reflect the reality of their lives – their context and rhythm, stories and visions, although at its heart, as Christian worship, will be the Scripture and the Breaking of Bread. It may be an informal meal in a house or pub; it may be related to work or leisure; it may use all manner of media or have a stark simplicity; it may be connected to a dispersed community like the Northumbrian Community or be focused on the annual highlight of Greenbelt; it may be in a large crowd meeting in some arena or theatre, or a dozen hidden away in the security of their retreat. It is possible to learn from the many stories that are now being told, though each, to be authentic, will be its own story.

Last, it is important that all this spills out into the personal prayer of the Christian community. Corporate worship is the framework for the scattered life of the Church through the week and in the wider community. Ways can be found to strengthen each other in intercessory prayer. There are many ways by which people can be reminded of God's presence: the wayside shrine, the angelus, or the cross or text in the house. Some people keep birthday calendars or diaries. For the Jews this is the function of the *mezuzah*, containing the *Shema,* attached to the door of the house, a reminder that God is at their coming in and going out (Psalm 121.8).

> Hear, O Israel; The LORD is our God, the LORD alone. You shall love the LORD your God with all your heart, and with all your soul, and with all your might. (Deuteronomy 6.4–5)

Bibliography

Introduction: community work and the churches

Church-related community work

Addy, Tony (ed.), 1990. *Community Work in the New Context*. Manchester, William Temple Foundation.

Addy, Tony, 1989. *Managing the Agenda: Christian reflection on mission and community work*. London, British Council of Churches.

Ballard, Paul (ed.), 1990. *Issues in Church Related Community Work*. HOLI 6. Cardiff, Pastoral Studies, Cardiff University.

Ballard, Paul and Redfern, Alistair (eds), 1990. 'Community Work in the Church.' *Christian Action Journal*, Winter 1989/90.

Godfrey, Wendy (ed.), 1985. *Down to Earth: stories of church based community work*. London, British Council of Churches.

Salmon, Harry, 1977. *Working with People: examples of community development*. London, Methodist Home Mission.

Reports (in chronological order)

Community Work and the Churches. 1976. London, British Council of Churches.

Involvement in Community: a Christian contribution. 1980. Manchester, William Temple Foundation.

Faith in the City. 1985. London, Archbishop's Commission on Urban Priority Areas, Church House.

The Church and Community Work. 1988. London, Board of Social Responsibility, Church of England.

Sedgwick, Peter (ed.), 1995. *God in the City*. The Archbishops' Urban Theology Group, London, Mowbray.

The Common Good and the Catholic Church's Social Teaching. 1996. London, Catholic Bishops' Conference of England and Wales.

The Cities – a Methodist report. 1997. London, NCH Action for Children.

Faithful Cities – a call for celebration, vision and justice. 2006. Commission on Urban Life and Faith, London, Methodist Publishing House and Church House Publishing.

The emergence of community work

Batten, T. R. and Madge, 1967. *The Non-Directive Approach in Group and Community Work*. London, OUP.

Henderson, P. and Thomas, D. N. (eds), 1981. *Readings in Community Work*. London, Allen and Unwin.

Thomas, D. N., 1983. *The Making of Community Work*. London, Allen and Unwin.

Reports (in chronological order)

Gulbenkian Foundation reports:

Younghusband, Eileen, 1968. *Community Work and Social Change*. London, Longman.

Community Work Group, 1973. *Current Issues in Community Work: a study*. London, Routledge and Kegan Paul.

Milsom report, 1969. *Youth and Community Work in the 70s*. London, HMSO.

Social Exclusion Unit, 2001. *A New Commitment to Neighbourhood Renewal*. London, HMSO.

White Paper, 2000. *Our Towns and Cities – the future*. London, DETR.

Background references

Cahoore, Lawrence, 2002. *From Modernism to Post-Modernism*. Oxford, Blackwell.

Davie, Grace, 1994. *Religion in Britain since 1945: believing without belonging*. Oxford, Blackwell.

Davie, Grace, 2000. *Religion in Europe: a memory mutates*. Oxford, Oxford University Press.

Fowler, James, 1996. *Faithful Change: the personal and public challenges of post-modern life*. Nashville, Abingdon.

Garratt, Chris and Rodrigues, Chris, 2004. *Introducing Modernism*. London, Icon.

Garratt, Chris and Appignanesi, Renard, 2003. *Introducing Post-modernism*. London, Icon.

Harvey, David, 1990. *The Condition of Postmodernity: an enquiry into the origins of cultural change*. Oxford, Blackwell.

Jacobs, Sidney and Popple, Keith (eds), 1994. *Community Work in the 1990s*. Nottingham, Spokesman.

Soja, Edward W., 2000. *Postmetropolis: crucial studies of cities and regions*. Oxford, Blackwell.

1 The elusive search for community

Discussions of community etc.

Atherton, John, 2003. *Marginalization*. London, SCM Press.
Bauman, Zygmunt, 2000. *Community: seeking safety in an insecure world*. Cambridge, Polity.
Cox, Harvey, 1965. *The Secular City*. London, SCM Press.
Dalley, Gillian, 1988. *Ideologies of Caring*. London, Macmillan.
Day, Graham, 2006. *Community and Everyday Life*. London, Routledge.
Delanty, Gerard, 2003. *Community*. London, Routledge.
Erikson, Erik, 1995. *Childhood and Society*. London, Vintage.
Etzioni, Amitai (ed.), 1998. *The Essential Communitarian Reader*. Lanham, Rowman and Littlefield.
Fromm, Erich, 2001. *The Fear of Freedom*. London, Routledge.
Fromm, Erich, 2002. *The Sane Society*. London, Routledge.
Hills, John, Le Grand, Julian and Piachaud, David (eds), 2002. *Understanding Social Exclusion*. Oxford, Oxford University Press.
Hopper, Paul, 2003. *Rebuilding Community in an Age of Individualism*. Aldershot, Ashgate.
Loughran, Keith, 2003. *The Idea of Community, Social Policy and the Self*. Belfast, APJ Publications.
Morisy, Ann, 2004. *Journeying out: a new approach to Christian mission*. London, Morehouse.
Newby, Howard, 1980. *Community*. Milton Keynes, Open University.
Payne, Malcolm, 1995. *Social Work and Community Care*. Basingstoke, Macmillan.
Plant, Raymond, 1974. *Community and Ideology*. London, Routledge and Kegan Paul.
Putnam, Robert D., 2000. *Bowling Alone: the collapse and revival of American communities*. New York, Simon and Schuster.
Taylor, Peter, 2005. *Who are the Capacity Builders?* London, Community Development Foundation.

Theological commentary

Baker, Chris and Skinner Hannah, 2005. *Telling Stories: how churches are responding to social capital*. Manchester, William Temple Foundation.
Beasley-Murray, George, 1986. *Jesus and the Kingdom*. Exeter, Paternoster.

Cunningham, David S., 1998. *These Three are One: the practice of Trinitarian theology*. Oxford, Blackwell.
Fiddes, Paul S., 2000. *Participating in God: a pastoral doctrine of the Trinity*. London, Darton, Longman and Todd.
Macquarrie, John, 1973. *The Concept of Peace*. London, SCM Press.
McFadyen, Alistair I., 1990. *The Call to Personhood: a Christian theology of the individual in social relationships*. Cambridge, Cambridge University Press.
Migliore, Daniel L., 2004. *Faith Seeking Understanding: an introduction to Christian Theology*. Grand Rapids, Eerdmans.
Ward, Pete, 2002. *Liquid Church*. Carlisle, Paternoster.
Zizoulas, John D., 1985. *Being as Communion*. London, Darton, Longman and Todd.

2 Community work and mission

Abraham, William, 1989. *The Logic of Evangelism*. London, Hodder and Stoughton.
Archbishops' Council, 2004. *A Mission-Shaped Church*. London, Church House Publishing.
Baker, Chris and Skinner, Hannah, 2006. *Faith in Action: the dynamics between spiritual and religious capital*. Manchester, William Temple Foundation.
Barrow, Simon and Smith, Graeme (eds), 2001. *Christian Mission in Western Society*. London, Churches Together in Britain and Ireland.
Bauckham, Richard, 2003. *The Bible and Mission*. Carlisle, Paternoster.
Beasley, Mary, 1997. *Mission on the Margins*. Cambridge, Lutterworth.
Bevans, Staphen B. 2000. *Models of Contextual Theology*. Maryknoll, Orbis Books.
Bevans, Staphen B. and Schroeder, Roger P., 2004. *Constants in Context: a theology of mission for today*. Maryknoll, Orbis Books.
Bonhoeffer, Dietrich, 1967. *Letters and Papers from Prison*. London, SCM Press.
Bosch, David J., 1991. *Transforming Mission: paradigm shifts in the theology of mission*. Maryknoll, Orbis Books.
Brewin, Kester, 2004. *The Complex Christ: signs of emergence in the urban church*. London, SPCK.
Chalke, Steve and Watkis, Anthony, 2006. *Intelligent Church: a journey towards Christ-centred community*. Grand Rapids, Zondervan.

Churches Together in Britain and Ireland, 2006. *Changing Mission: learning from the newer churches*. London, CTBI.

Cottrell, Stephen, 2006. *From the Abundance of the Heart: Catholic evangelism for all Christians*. London, Darton, Longman and Todd.

Davey, Andrew, 2001. *Urban Christianity and the Global Order*. London, SPCK.

Finney, John, 2004. *Emerging Evangelism*. London, Darton, Longman and Todd.

Fuder, John, 2005. *Heart for the City: effective ministries to the urban community*. Chicago, Moody.

Fuellenbach, John, 2002. *Church: Community for the Kingdom*. Maryknoll, Orbis Books.

Gibbs, Eddie and Bolger, Ryan K., 2006. *Emerging Churches: creating Christian community in postmodern cultures*. London, SPCK.

Glasson, Barbara, 2006. *Mixed-Up Blessing: a new encounter with being Church*. Peterborough, Inspire.

Goodliff, Paul, 1998. *Care in a Confused Climate: pastoral care in postmodern culture*. London, Darton, Longman and Todd.

Grundy, Malcolm, 1998. *Understanding Congregations: A new shape for the local church*. London, Mowbray.

Gutiérrez, Gustavo, 1974. *A Theology of Liberation*. London, SCM Press.

Hollenweger, Walter, 1968. *The Missionary Structure of the Congregation*. Geneva, World Council of Churches.

Kirk, J. Andrew, 1999. *What is Mission? theological explorations*. London, Darton, Longman and Todd.

Kirk, J. Andrew, 2006. *Mission Under Scrutiny: confronting current challenges*. London, Darton, Longman and Todd.

Lausanne Committee for World Evangelisation, 1989. *The Manila Manifesto: an elaboration of the Lausanne Covenant fifteen years earlier*.

McGavran, Donald, 1959. *How Churches Grow*. New York, Friendship Press.

Morisy, Ann, 1997. *Beyond the Good Samaritan: community ministry and mission*. London, Mowbray.

Morisy, Ann, 2004. *Journeying Out: a new approach to Christian mission*. London, Morehouse.

Moynagh, Michael, 2001. *Changing World, Changing Church*. London, Monarch.

Newbigin, Lesslie, 1978. *The Open Secret*. London, SPCK.

Scherer, James A. and Bevans, Stephen B. (eds), 1992. *New Directions in Mission and Evangelism, 1. Basic Statements 1974–91*. Maryknoll, Orbis Books.

Stott, John, 1975. *Christian Mission in the Modern World*. London, Falcon.

Taylor, John V., 1972. *The Go-Between God: The Holy Spirit in the Christian mission*. London, SCM Press.

Thangaraj, M. Thomas, 1999. *The Common Task: a theology of Christian mission*. Nashville, Abingdon.

Thomas, Norman (ed.), 1995. *Readings in World Mission*. London, SPCK.

Tomlin, Graham, 2004. *The Provocative Church*. London, SPCK.

Torry, Malcolm, 2007. *Regeneration: new ways of being Church in changing communities*. Norwich, Canterbury Press.

Warren, Robert, 1995. *Being Human, Being Church: spirituality and mission in the local church*. London, Marshall Pickering.

World Council of Churches, 1967. *The Church for Others and the Church for the World*. Geneva, WCC.

World Council of Churches, 1982. *Ecumenical Affirmation: Mission and Evangelism*. Geneva, WCC.

3 Models and modes of community work

Briscoe, C. and Thomas, David N., 1977. *Community Development and Renewal Issues*. London, Allen and Unwin.

Finneron, Doreen, 1993. *Faith in Community Development*. Manchester, Manchester University Press.

Finneron, Doreen *et al.*, 2001. *Challenging Communities: church related community development and neighbourhood renewal*. Durham, Churches' Community Work Alliance.

Francis, David and Henderson, Paul, 2000. *Community Development and Renewal Issues*. London, Community Development Foundation.

Freire, Paulo, 1974. *Education for Critical Consciousness*. London, Sheed and Ward.

Freire, Paulo, 1993. *Pedagogy of the Oppressed*. Harmondsworth, Penguin.

Gilchrist, Alison, 2004. *The Well-Connected Community: a networking approach*. Bristol, Policy Press.

Gilchrist, Alison, 2006. *Community Developing and Networking*. London, Community Development Foundation.

Grundy, Malcolm, 1995. *Community Work: a handbook for volunteer groups and local churches.* London, Mowbray.
Handy, Charles, 1988. *Understanding Voluntary Organisations.* Harmondsworth, Penguin.
Handy, Charles, 1993. *Understanding Organisations.* Harmondsworth, Penguin.
Henderson, Paul and Thomas, David N., 1974. *Skills in Community Work.* London, Routledge and Kegan Paul.
Ledwith, Margaret, 2005. *Community Development: a critical approach.* Bristol, Policy Press.
Lovell, George, 1972. *The Church and Community Development.* London, Grail.
Lovell, George, 1982. *Human and Religious Factors in Church and Community Work.* London, Grail.
Lovell, George, 1995. *Analysis and Design.* Peterborough, Epworth.
Mears, Robin, 1994. *Community Care: policy and practice.* Basingstoke, Methuen.
Milson, Fred, 1974. *An Introduction to Community Work.* London, Routledge and Kegan Paul.
Payne, Malcolm, 1995. *Social Work and Community Care.* Basingstoke, Macmillan.
Rogers, Carl, 1967. *On Becoming a Person.* London, Constable.
Rogers, Carl, 1980. *A Way of Being.* Boston, Houghton Mifflin.
Skeffington Report. 1969. London, HMSO.
Taylor, Peter, 2001. *Community Development in Practice.* London, Community Development Foundation.
Thompson, Neil and Thompson, Sue, 2005. *Community Care.* Lyme Regis, Russell House.
Twelvetrees, Alan, 2000. *Community Work.* London, Macmillan.

4 Turning towards the community

Making a community profile

Adirondack, Sandy, 2000. *Just about Managing.* London, London Voluntary Service Council.
Bell, Diane, Caplan, Pat and Karim, Wazir Jahan (eds), 1993. *Gendered Fields: women, men and ethnology.* London, Routledge.
Bell, Judith, 1999. *Doing your research project.* Milton Keynes, Open University Press.

Gilbert, Nigel (ed.), 2001. *Researching Social Life.* London, Sage Publications.

Hammersley, Martin and Atkinson, Paul, 1995. *Ethnography: principles and practice.* London, Routledge.

Hawtin, Murray, Hughes, Geraint and Percy-Smith, Janie, 1994. *Community Profiling: auditing social needs.* Milton Keynes, Open University Press.

Henderson, Paul and Thomas, David N. (eds), 1980. *Skills in Neighbourhood Work.* London, Unwin Hyman.

Holland, Joe and Henriot, Peter, 1992. *Social Analysis: linking faith and justice.* Maryknoll, Orbis Books.

Kane, Eileen, 1995. *Doing Your Own Research: how to do basic descriptive research in the social sciences and the humanities.* London, Marion Boyars.

Levitas, Ruth and Guy, Will (eds), 1996. *Interpreting Official Statistics.* London, Routledge.

Neumann, W. Lawrence, 1999. *Social Research Methods.* Boston, Allyn and Bacon.

Shipman, Marten, 1997. *The Limitations of Social Research.* London, Longman.

Silverman, David, 2002. *Interpreting Qualitative Data: methods for analysing talk, text and interaction.* London, Routledge.

Websites

AVEC Resources. Kensington Square, London. 020 8868 0628/2195.

Doing Community Research (downloadable on web): <www.bassac.org.uk>.

ENSURE: methods for getting to know the neighbourhood: <www.ensure.org>.

Faithworks, 2007. *Community Audit.* <www.faithworks.info>. 020 7450 9052.

Government statistics: <www.neighbourhood.gov.uk>; <www.statistics.gov.uk/census>.

Ordnance Survey: <www.ordnancesurvey.co.uk/oswebsite>.

Parish audit

Ammerman, Nancy *et al.* (eds), 1998. *Studying Congregations: a new handbook.* Nashville, Abingdon.

Adaptability CD: A diagnostic tool for churches to assess their current level of community action <www.eauk.org.uk>.

ARVAC, 2001. *Community Research: getting started; a resource pack for community groups* (Association for Research in the Voluntary and Community Sector).

Cameron, Helen, *et al.*, 2005. *Studying Local Churches: a handbook.* London, SCM Press.

Faithworks, 2002. *Church Audit.* <www.faithworks.info>.

Guest, Mathew, Tusting, Karin and Woodhead, Linda (eds), 2004. *Congregational Studies in the UK: Christianity in a post-Christian context.* Andover, Ashgate.

Rural communities

Bowden, Andrew, 2003. *Ministry in the Countryside.* London, Continuum.

Faith in the Countryside, 1990. A report to the Archbishops of Canterbury and York. 1990. Norwich, Churchman.

Suburbia

Brown, Malcolm, 2005. *Faith in Suburbia.* Edinburgh, Contact Pastoral Trust.

Thorns, David C., 1972. *Suburbia.* London, McGibbons and Key.

5 Living with ethnic, cultural and religious diversity

General

Abercrombie, Nicholas *et al.* (eds), 2000. *Contempory British Society.* London, Polity Press.

Blakemore, Ken and Drake, Robert, 1996. *Understanding Equal Opportunity Policies.* Hemel Hempstead, Prentice Hall.

Davies, Martin (ed.), 2000. *The Blackwell Encyclopaedia of Social Work.* Oxford, Blackwell.

Dominelli, Lena, 2002. *Anti-Oppressive Social Work Theory and Practice.* London, Palgrave.

Disability, difference and social exclusion

Askonas, Peter and Stewart, Angus (eds), 2000. *Social Inclusion: possibilities and tensions.* Basingstoke, Macmillan.

Dalrymple, Jane and Burke, Beverley, 1995. *Anti-Oppressive Practice: social care and the law.* Milton Keynes, Open University.

Hewitt, Patricia, 1989. *The Abuse of Power: civil liberties in the UK.* Oxford, Robertson.

Hills, John (ed.), 2000. *Understanding Social Exclusion*. Oxford, Oxford University Press.

Hope, Anne and Timmel, Sally, 1994. *Training for Transformation: a handbook for community workers Vols 1–4*. London, ITDG Publishing.

Kallen, Evelyn, 2004. *Social Inequality and Social Injustice: a human rights perspective*. London, Palgrave.

Ledwith, M., 1997. *Participating in Transformation: towards a working model of community empowerment*. Birmingham, Venture.

Oliver, Mike, 1996. *Understanding Disability*. Basingstoke, Macmillan.

Thomas, Erica, 2004. *Respect!: a guide to understanding anti-oppressive practice for youth workers and those involved in community work*. Preston, HLB Associates. <hlb@hlbassociation.plus.com>

Thompson, Neil, 2001. *Anti-Discriminatory Practice*. London, British Association of Social Workers Practical Social Work, Palgrave.

Thompson, Neil, 2003. *Promoting Equality: challenging discrimination and oppression*. London, Palgrave.

Racism

Donald, James and Rattansi, Ali, 1992. *Race, Culture and Difference*. Milton Keynes, Open University Press.

Frederickson, George M., 2002. *Racism: a short history*. Princeton, Princeton University Press.

Haslam, David, 1996. *Race for the Millennium: a challenge to Church and society*. London, Church House Publishing.

Lartey, E., 2006. *Pastoral Trends in an Inter-Cultural World*. Peterborough, Epworth.

Leech, Kenneth, 2005. *Race: changing society and the churches*. London, SPCK.

Radcliffe, Peter, 2004. *'Race', Ethnicity and Difference: imaging the inclusive society*. Milton Keynes, Open University Press.

Resources

Ubuntu <www.fcdl.org.uk>. A network for black perspectives in community development.

Gender

Briggs, Richard, 2001. *Gender and the New Testament: six proposals for interpretation*. Cambridge, Grove Books.

King, Ursula, 1994. *Feminist Theology from the Third World: a reader*. London, SPCK.

Loades, Ann, 1990. *Feminist Theology: a reader*. London, SPCK.
Parsons, Susan, F. (ed.), 2000. *Challenging Women's Orthodoxies in the Context of Faith*. Aldershot, Ashgate.
Ruether, Rosemary, 1992. *Sexism and God-Talk*. London, SCM Press.

Asylum-seekers and refugees

Bradstock, Andrew (ed.), 2003. *Asylum Voices: issues of seeking asylum in the UK*. London, Churches Together in Britain and Ireland.
Burns, Stephen, 2004. *Welcoming Asylum Seekers*. Cambridge, Grove Books, Ethics Series.
Ruther, Jill, 1998. *Refugees: a resource for primary schools*. London, Refugee Council.

Resources

RADAR CD-Rom: Refugee Organisations in the UK.
Refugee Council: publications on <books@refugeecouncil.org.uk>.

Other faiths

Cole, W. Owen *et al.*, 2004. *Six World Faiths*. London, Continuum.
D'Costa, Gavin, 2000. *The Meeting of Religions and the Trinity*. Edinburgh, T&T Clark.
Disbrey, Claire, 2004. *Listening to People of Other Faiths*. Oxford, Bible Reading Fellowship.
Glaser, Ida, 2005. *The Bible and Other Faiths: what does the Lord require of us?* Leicester, Inter-Varsity Press.
Goldsmith, Martin, 2003. *What about Other Faiths? is Jesus Christ the only way to God?* London, Hodder and Stoughton.
Häring, Hermann, Martin Soskice, Janet and Wilfred, Felix (eds), 2003. *Learning from Other Faiths*. London, SCM Press.
Korn, Eugene B. and Pawlikowski, John T. (eds), 2005. *Two Faiths, One Covenant? Jewish and Christian identity in the presence of the other*. Oxford: Rowman and Littlefield.

Resources

Inter Faith Network: <www.interfaith.org.uk> 020 7931 7766. Relations between all the major faiths in Britain.
Ministry among Asians in Britain (MAB): 0121 643 7771. Churches in cross-cultural work.

Ageism

Bytheway, Bill, 1995. *Ageism.* Milton Keynes, Open University.

Church of England, Board of Social Responsibility, 1990. *Ageing.* London, Church House Publishing.

House of Commons, Health Committee, 2003–04. *Elder Abuse: Second Report of Session.* Vol. 1.

Johnson, Julia and Slater, Robert (eds), 1993. *Ageing and Later Life.* London, Sage.

Nelson, Todd (ed.), 2002. *Ageism: stereotyping and prejudice against older persons.* Cambridge, MIT Press.

Wyn, Johanna and White, Rob, 1997. *Rethinking Youth.* London, Sage.

Resources

A Cream Cracker under the Settee (Thora Hird). Alan Bennett, *Talking Heads.* BBC, 1997. BBC Worldwide Ltd.

Action on Elder Abuse, Astral House, 1268 London Road, SW16 4ER. 020 8765 4074. <www.elderabuse.org.uk>.

Age Concern. <www.ageconcern.org.uk> 0800 328 0894. Local services as well as influencing public opinion and government.

Dad (Richard Briers and Kevin Whately). Lucy Gannon. BBC, February 2005. BBC Worldwide Ltd.

Information Services for Profit. Useful in relation to the law of employment etc. <www.is4profit.com/businessadvice/employment/age-discrimination>.

Iris (Judi Dench, Jim Broadbent and Kate Winslet). BBC Films, 2001. Buena Vista Home Entertainment Ltd.

Should I Worry about Aging? (Richard Hammond). BBC, August 2005. BBC Worldwide Ltd.

6 Working with allies

Funding

Lottery grants

The Active Communities Development Fund: to enable people with disabilities, from ethnic minorities, women and girls, and those on low incomes to participate in sports. (Sport England, 0845 764969, <www.sportengland.org.uk>.)

Awards for All: small grants (£500 and £5,000). England only, with less than £15,000 income per annum. Open. <www.awardsforall.org.uk>.

Community Capital Programme Funding. (For sport charities, contact Sport England.)

Community Fund: the big funding stream, supporting groups that work for disadvantaged communities. 020 7747 5299. <enquiries@ community-fund.org.uk>.

The Heritage Lottery Fund: conservation and heritage schemes; listed buildings. <www.hlf.org.uk>.

The Lottery Arts Fund: administered by the Arts Council. May help, e.g., with the repair of organs which are used for concert use. <www. artscouncil.org.uk>.

The Main Grants Programme (greater than £50,000): will fund church projects, but must include heritage benefit to wider communities such as access to public places and education. <www.hlf.org.uk>.

The Repair Scheme for Places of Worship: with English Heritage; schemes in Wales, Scotland and Northern Ireland. <www.english-heritage.org.uk>.

Your Heritage: grants up to £50,000 for smaller non-structural conservation of features but not furniture. <www.hlf.org.uk>.

Government schemes

English Heritage (<www.english-heritage.org.uk>); CADW (Welsh Historic Monuments: <www.CADW.wales.gov.uk>); Historic Scotland (<www.historic-scotland.gov.uk>); Northern Ireland Office Historic Monuments and Buildings Branch (<www.opsi.gov.uk>) Church buildings.

The Landfill Tax Scheme: groups beginning a community scheme. <www.ltcs.org.uk>.

Listed Places of Worship Grant Scheme (0845 601 5945) <www. lpwscheme.org.uk>.

Local Strategic Partnerships: LSP Team of the Neighbourhood Renewal Unit: <nrulspteam@odpm.gsi.gov.uk>. Contact your local *Government Office (GOs)*, or <www.neighbourhood.gov>.

The Single Regeneration Budget and the Regional Development Agency: <www.communities.gov.uk>.

Government funding for the voluntary and community sectors

Community Chests: <www.governmentfunding.org.uk> and <www. volcomgrants.gov.uk>.

The European Union also makes grants, but you need to be persistent to succeed; they may claw back unspent grants. Search from <www.direct.gov.uk>.

Scottish Community Action Research Fund (SCARF) <www.communitiesscotland.gov.uk>.

Sure Start: funding work with under 5s – <www.surestart.gov.uk>. 0845 602 2260.

Other useful sources for grants

Age Concern England: <www.ageconcern.org.uk> 020 8765 7738.

All Churches Trust Limited: <www.ecclesiastical.org.uk> 01452 528533.

Biffa: <www.biffa.co.uk/biffaward>.

The Baring Foundation: <www.baringfoundation.org.uk>.

The Church of England: <www.churchcare.co.uk>.

The Church Urban Fund: <www.cuf.org.uk> 0845 275 000.

The Countryside Agency: <www.countryside.org.uk> 0870 333 0170.

Help the Aged: 01258 458 406.

Scottish Churches Community Trust: <www.scct.org.uk> 0141 336 3766.

Guides and other background material

Ali, Moi, 1996. *The DIY Guide to Marketing: for small charities, voluntary organisations and community groups*. London, Directory of Social Change.

BURA: British Urban Regeneration Association. <www.bura.org.uk>.

Communities in Crisis, 1985. Oxford, Ruskin College and Manchester, William Temple Foundation.

Community Research: getting started; a resource pack for community groups. Association for Research in the Voluntary and Community Sector.

Davison, Ann, 1993. *Grants for Europe: how to get money and influence policy*. London, ERICA National Council for Voluntary Organizations.

Directory of Social Change: The Directory of Grant Making Trusts, 2005–06. West Malling, Caritas Aid Foundation. Available in most central libraries.

Durran, Maggie, 2003. *The UK Church Fundraising Handbook: a practical manual and directory of sources*. Norwich, Canterbury Press.

Fisher, Jenny and Sarkar, Rupa, 2006. *The LSP Guide 2006 3rd Edition: a handy guide to getting involved for voluntary and community groups*. London, Urban Forum <www.urbanforum.org.uk> and Community Development Foundation.

Gilchrist, Alison with Rauf, Tanwir, 2006. *Community Development and Networking*. London, Community Development Foundation.
The Green Fish Partnership, *Factpack*. Manchester, The Green Fish Partnership 0161 236 3206 <www.vamanchester.org.uk>.
Hanvey, Chris and Philpot, Terry (eds), 1996. *Sweet Charity: the role and working of voluntary organisations*. London, Routledge.
London Voluntary Service Council, 1990. *Voluntary but Not Amateur: a guide to the law for voluntary organisations and community groups*. London.
Mawson, Andrew, *et al.*, *One Church, 100 Uses: The National Agency for the Creative Transformation of Churches*. London, Lekker Design, Bromley by Bow Centre.
Norton, Michael, 1992. *Writing Better Fundraising Applications: a practical guide with worked examples, exercises and ideas for worksheets*. London, The Directory of Social Change in association with the Institute of Charity Fundraising Managers.
The Purple Book for Planning Projects. Part 1 Finding Out; Part 2 The Planning Process; Part 3 Running; Part 4 Managing. London, Southwark Diocese Board for Church in Society.
Voluntary Action Councils, in local authorities throughout UK. Membership is open to voluntary sector.

7 Working with volunteers

Books etc.

McCulloch, Lindsay, 2001. *Opening Doors: an accreditation guide for the voluntary sector*. RSA Project 2001, in partnership with NACVS. Free from <www.voluntarysectorskills.org.uk>.
Robson, P., Locke, M. and Dawson, J., 1997. *User Involvement in the Control of Voluntary Organisations*. Bristol, Policy Press. <www.jrf.org.uk/knowledge/findings/socialcare>.
VSNTO, 2001. *Would you credit it? A guide to S/NVQs for the voluntary sector*, free, from <www.voluntarysectorskills.org.uk>.

Resources

Some Christian and faith-based agencies and organizations

Barnardos: <www.barnardos.org.uk> 020 8550 8822.
Caritas-social action: <www.caritas-socialaction.org.uk> 020 7901 4875.

The Children's Society: <www.childrenssociety.org.uk>.

Christian Action Networks (CANs) Evangelical Alliance: <www.eauk.org.uk> 020 7207 2152.

Church Action on Poverty (CAP): <www.church-poverty.org.uk> 0161 236 9321.

Churches Community Work Alliance (CCWA) (A network of CTBI): <www.ccwa.org.uk> 0191 334 3346.

European Contact Group on Industrial Urban Mission (ECG): <www.ecg.ecn.cz>.

Faith Based Regeneration Network: <fbrnuk@aol.com> 020 8947 6160.

Luther King Open College, Partnership for Theological Education: Luther King House, Brighton Grove, Rusholme, Manchester M14 5JP <www.ptem.org.uk> 0161 224 4381.

NCH Action for Children: <www.nch.org.uk> 85 Highbury Park, London N5 1UD.

The Shaftesbury Society: <www.shaftesbury.org> 0845 330 6033.

Spurgeon's Child Care: <www.ncvcco.org/information> 74 Wellingborough Road, Rushden, Northamptonshire N10 9TY 01933 412412.

Training for Learning and Serving (TLS): Lite and level 1/2 courses in Community Work: The United Reformed Church, 86 Tavistock Place, London WC1H 9RT.

Other resources

Active Communities Unit, Home Office: <www.homeoffice.gov.uk/acu> 020 7035 5328.

Association of Independent Credit Unions Ltd: <01274 652042>.

Associations of British Credit Unions Ltd: <www.abcul.org> 0161 832 3694.

Communities Scotland: <www.communitiesscotland.gov.uk> 0131 313 0044. Part of the Scottish Executive working for housing and regeneration in Scotland.

Community Action Network (CAN): <www.can-online.org.uk> 0207 401 5310. A mutual learning and support network for social entrepreneurs. It aims to connect people using state of the art technology as a tool for communication.

Community Development Foundation: Unit 5, Angel Gate, 320 City Road, London EC1V 2PT. 020 7612 5449.

Community Work Forum (CWF): <www.paulo.org.uk or www.fcdl.org.uk>.

Federation for Community Development Learning: <www.fcdl.org.uk>.

Federation of City Farms and Community Gardens: <www.farmgarden/org.uk> 0117 9231 800.

Learning and Skills Council: Cheylesmore House, Quinton Road, Coventry CV1 2WT Helpline: 0870 900 6800 <info@lsc.gov.uk>; <www.lsc.gov.uk>.

National Council for Voluntary Organisations (NCVO): <www.ncvo-vol.org.uk> 020 7713 6161.

National Council for Voluntary Services (NACVS): <www.nacvs.org.uk> 0114 278 6636.

National Institute for Adult and Continuing Education (NIACE): <www.niace.org.uk> 0116 204 4200.

National Open College Network (OCN): The Quadrant, Parkway Business Park, 99 Parkway Avenue, Sheffield S9 4WG 0114 227 0500 <nocn@nocn.org.uk>, <www.nocn.org.uk/>.

Partnership at Work: <www.partnershipatwork.org.uk> 0121 244 5969.

PAULO: <www.paulo.org.uk> The Standards Setting Body (formerly the National Training Organization) for the Community-Based Learning and Development sector.

Personal Development Unit: University of Wales, Lampeter <www.volstudy.ac.skills>.

Qualifications and Curriculum Authority: 83 Piccadilly, London W1J 8QA 020 7509 5556 <info@qca.org.uk>; <www.qca.org.uk/>.

Scottish Poverty Alliance: <www.povertyalliance.org> 0141 353 0440.

Scottish Qualification Authority: Hanover House, 24 Douglas Street, Glasgow G2 7NQ 0141 248 7900 <customer@sqa.org.uk>; <www.sqa.org.uk/>.

Volunteering England Information Service: Regent's Wharf, 8 All Saints Street, London N1 9RL 0800 028 3304 <Information@volunteering-england.org>; <www.volunteering.org.uk>.

Wales Council for Voluntary Action: 029 2043 1700 <www.wcva.org.uk>.

8 The community leader

Styles of leadership

Adair, John, 2003. *Effective strategic leadership*. London, Pan.

Allen, Roger E. and Allen, Stephen D., 1997. *Winnie-the-Pooh on Problem Solving: in which Pooh, Piglet and friends explore how to solve problems so you can too*. London, Methuen.

Anderson, Keith R. and Pease, Randy D., 1999. *Spiritual Mentoring: a guide for seeking and giving direction*. Guildford, Eagle.

Batsleer, Julian, *et al.* (eds), 1992. *Issues in Voluntary and Non-Profit Management*. Wokingham, Addison-Wesley.

Beasley-Murray, Paul, 1998. *Power for God's Sake: power and abuse in the local church*. Carlisle, Paternoster.

Bird, Malcolm, 1992. *Effective Leadership: a practical guide to leading your team to success*. London, BBC Books.

Blanchard, Kenneth, 1994. *Leadership and the One Minute Manager*. London, HarperCollins.

Brown, Rosalind and Cocksworth, Christopher, 2004. *Being a Priest Today: exploring priestly identity*. Cambridge MA, Cowley.

Channon, Gabriel, 1999. *Local Community Involvement: a handbook for good practice*. London, Community Development Federation.

Croft, Steven, 2002. *Transforming Communities: re-imagining the church for the 21st century*. London, Darton, Longman and Todd.

Croft, Steven and Walton, Roger, 2005. *Learning for Ministry*. London, Church House Publishing.

Doel, Mark and Sawdon, Catherine, 1999. *The Essential Group Worker: teaching and learning creative group work*. London, Jessica Kingsley.

Edmondson, Chris, 2002. *Fit to Lead: sustaining effective ministry in a changing world*. London, Darton, Longman and Todd.

Gill, Robin and Burke, Derek, 2002. *Strategic Church Leadership*. London, SPCK.

Gillen, Terry, 2002. *Leadership Skills for Boosting Performance*. London, Chartered Institute of Personnel and Development.

Grundy, Malcolm, 2007. *What's New in Church Leadership?* Norwich, Canterbury.

Hope, Anne and Timmel, Sally, 1990/99. *Training for Transformation: A Handbook for Community Workers*, Books 3/4. London, ITDG Publishing.

Kroehnert, Gary, 1999. *101 More Training Games*. New York, McGraw-Hill.

Lovell, George, 1996. *Avec: agency and approach*. Pinner, AVEC.

Lovell, George, 2000. *Consultancy, Ministry and Mission: a handbook for practitioners and work consultants in Christian organizations*. London, Burns and Oates.

Maslow, Abraham, 1968. *Towards a Psychology of Being*. Princeton NJ, Van Nostrand Reinhold.

Myers-Briggs Type Indicator. <www.personalitypathways.com/type_inventory.html> or <www.myersbriggs.org>.

Nelson, John (ed.), 1999. *Leading, Managing Ministering: challenging questions for Church and society*. Norwich, Canterbury.

Newstrom, John and Scannell, Edward, 1998. *The Big Book of Team Building Games: trust-building activities, team spirit exercises and other fun things to do*. London, McGraw-Hill.

Reason, Jacki, Hayes, Ruth and Forbes, Duncan, 2000. *Voluntary but not Amateur: a guide to the law for voluntary organisations and community groups*. London Voluntary Service Council.

Rossiter, J. and Summers, Steve, 2004. *Assets for Life*. London, United Reformed Church.

Stewart, Murray and Taylor, Marilyn, 1993. *Local government community leadership: the strategic role of the local authority*. Luton, Local Government Management Board.

Tidball, Derek, 1999. *Builders and Fools: leadership in the Bible way*. Leicester, IVP.

Widdicombe, Catherine, 2000. *Meetings that Work: a practical guide to team-working in groups*. Cambridge, Lutterworth.

Woolfe, Lorin, 2002. *The Bible on Leadership: from Moses to Matthew – management lessons for contemporary leaders*. New York, American Management Association.

Supervision and support

Coulshed, Veronica and Mullender, Audrey (eds), 2001. *Management in Social Work*. Basingstoke, Palgrave.

Foskett, John and Lyall, David, 1988. *Helping the Helpers: Supervision and Pastoral Care*. London, SPCK.

Hawkins, Peter and Shohet, Robin, 1997. *Supervision in the Helping Professions*. Oxford, Oxford University Press.

Morrison, Tony, 1997. *Staff Supervision in Social Care*. Brighton, Pavilion.

Pritchard, Jacki, 2005. *Good Practice in Supervision in Statutory and Voluntary Organisations*. London, Jessica Kingsley.

Spriggs, David, 1993. *Christian Leadership*. Swindon, Bible Society.

Ward, Frances, 2005. *Lifelong Learning: theological education and supervision*. London, SCM Press.

Professional courses in church-related community work

Dip. HE in Church and Community Work: Roehampton University of Surrey, Erasmus House, Roehampton Lane, London SW15 5PU. <enquiries@roehampton.ac.uk> 020 8392 3000.

Foundation and Honours Degrees in Contextual Theology (Community Work): Luther King Open College and/or Northern College, Partnership for Theological Education, Luther King House, Manchester M14 5JP. <www.ptem.org.uk> 0161 224 4381.

Conflict management

Crawley, John, 1992. *Constructive Conflict Management*. London, Nicholas Brealey.

Laurance, Linda and Radford, Anne, 1997. *Dealing with Disputes in Voluntary Organisations: an introduction*. London, National Council for Voluntary Organisations.

Salter, Brian and Langford-Wood, Naomi, 1998. *Dealing with Difficult People in a Week*. London, Hodder and Stoughton.

Management

Adirondack, Sandy, 2000. *Just about Managing*. London, London Voluntary Service Council.

Banks, Sarah *et al.*, 2003. *Managing Community Practice: principles, policies and programmes*. Bristol, Policy.

Belbin, Meredith, 2004. *Management Teams: why they succeed or fail*. Oxford, Butterworth-Heinemann.

Coulshead, Veronica and Mullender, Audrey, 2001. *Management and Social Work*. Basingstoke, Palgrave.

Handy, Charles, 1988. *Understanding Voluntary Organisations*. Harmondsworth, Penguin.

9 Spirituality in community participation

General

Ballard, Paul (ed.), 1990. *Issues in Church Related Community Work*. Cardiff, Pastoral Studies, Cardiff University.

Bonhoeffer, Dietrich, 1955. *Ethics*. London, SCM Press.

Dorr, Donal, 2006. *The Spirituality of Leadership*. Dublin, Columba.

Elliott, Charles, 1985. *Praying the Kingdom*. London, Darton, Longman and Todd.

Farley, Edward, 1980. *Theologia: fragmentation and unity in theological education*. New York, Fortress.

Hinton, Donald, 1984. *A Word in Season*. Redhill, National Christian Education Council.

Howard, Sue and Welbourn, David, 2004. *The Spirit at Work Phenomenon*. London, Azure.

Lawrence, Brother, 1968. *The Practice of the Presence of God*. London, Epworth.

Lynch, Gordon, 2002. *After Religion: Generation X and the search for meaning*. London, Darton, Longman and Todd.

Niebuhr, H. Richard, 1951. *Christ and Culture*. New York, Harper and Row.
Runcorn, D., 2006. *A Spirituality Workbook: a guide for explorers, pilgrims and seekers*. London, SPCK.
Savage, Sara *et al.*, 2006. *Making Sense of Generation Y: the world view of 15–25-year-olds*. London, Church House Publishing.
Schön, Donald, 1995. *The Reflective Practitioner*. Aldershot, Arena.
Sedgwick, Peter (ed.), 1995. *God in the City*. London, Mowbray.
Spriggs, David, 1993. *Christian Leadership*. Swindon, Bible Society.
Thornton, Martin, 1984. *Spiritual Direction*. London, SPCK.
Waller, R. and Ward, D. (eds), 1992. *An Introduction to Christian Spirituality*. London, SPCK.

Theological reflection

Bevans, Stephen, 2000. *Models of Contextual Theology*. Maryknoll, Orbis Books.
Graham, Elaine, Walton, Heather, Ward, Frances (eds), 2005. *Theological Reflection: Methods*. London, SCM Press.
Green, Laurie, 1990. *Let's Do Theology*. London, Mowbray.
Killen, Patricia O'Connell and de Beer, John, 1994. *The Art of Theological Reflection*. New York, Crossroad.
Osborne, L., 1988. *Dear Diary: an introduction to spiritual journalling*. Cambridge, Grove Books, Spirituality Series no. 25.
Reader, J., 1994. *Local Theology*. London, SPCK.
Thompson, Judith, 2007. *SCM Study Guide to Theological Reflection*. London, SCM Press.
Weaver, John, 2006. *Outside-in: theological reflection on life*. Oxford, Smyth and Helwys.

10 Worship in and for the community

Clark, Neville, 1960. *Call to Worship*. London, SCM Press.
Common Worship. 2000. London, Church House Publishing.
Draper, Brian and Draper, Kevin, 2000. *Refreshing Worship*. London, Bible Reading Fellowship.
Ellis, Robert, 2005. *Answering God*. Milton Keynes, Paternoster.
Gibbs, Eddie and Bolger, Ryan, 2006. *Emerging Churches*. Grand Rapids, Baker.
Jones, Cheslyn *et al.*, 1992. *The Study of Liturgy*. London, SPCK.
Murray, Stuart, 2006. *Changing Mission: learning from the newer churches*. London, CTBI.

Roman Missal, The, 1989. Newry, CBC Distributors.

Strafford, Tim, 2006. *Worship: window on the urban church*. London, SPCK.

Sykes, Stephen (ed.), 1997. *Holy, Holy, Holy: worshipping the trinitarian God*. London, Darton, Longman and Todd.

Tutu, Desmond, 1983. *Hope and Suffering*. London, Collins.

Ward, Pete, 2005. *Selling Worship*. Milton Keynes, Paternoster.

White, James F., 1990. *Introducing Christian Worship*. Nashville, Abingdon.

White, Susan J., 1997. *Groundwork of Christian Worship*. Peterborough, Epworth.

Willimon, William H., 1979. *Worship and Pastoral Care*. Nashville, Abingdon.

Glossary

Acknowledgement is made of material from *Assets for Life* (URC 2004) and *What Is Community Development?* (Federation for Community Development Learning n.d.; see Chapter 7).

Additionality: a way of measuring the benefits of a project which highlights the changes brought about which would not have occurred if the project hadn't taken place.

Anti-discriminatory practice: working in a way that actively removes barriers that might prevent people or groups from taking part.

Anti-poverty strategies (APS): an attempt at a co-ordinated approach to tackling poverty, including programmes to help people claim benefits, manage debt, have access to low interest small loans and better access to social work and housing agencies.

Area-based regeneration: in some areas, problems of economic, social and environmental dereliction combine to lock local communities into a vicious cycle of exclusion. Area-based initiatives encourage a range of partners to work together, targeting their combined resources at specific objectives in order to improve the quality of life in these areas.

Area Investment Frameworks (AIFs): set out the regeneration priorities for an area with the aim of targeting funding from regional development agencies (see RDAs). AIFs are developed by partnerships of local and regional agencies.

Baseline: a measurement of the starting conditions before a programme is undertaken, to be compared later with more up-to-date figures.

Best Value: a Government scheme to encourage local authorities to consult much more effectively and efficiently about the services they provide or purchase.

Building Communities Initiative: managed by Free Form Arts Trust, which encourages local communities to participate in housing regeneration projects. Facilitated by Free Form Design and Technical Services. <www.freeform.org.uk>.

Business Broker Schemes: Local Strategic Partnerships are being invited to bid for these to assist businesses in maximizing their contribution to neighbourhood renewal. Business in the Community and the British Chambers of Commerce are co-ordinating the project. <www.neighbourhood.gov.uk/brokers.asp>.

Capacity building: development work that strengthens the ability of community organizations to build their structures, systems, people and skills so that they are better able to define and achieve their objectives, engage in consultation and planning, manage their community projects and take part in partnerships and community enterprises. It includes aspects of training, organizational and personal development and resource building, organized in a planned and self-conscious manner reflecting principles of empowerment and equality.

City Pride: citywide partnerships, launched in 1993, to enhance the cities of Birmingham, London and Manchester.

Communities First: a Welsh Assembly programme to establish 100 partnerships in areas of deprivation across Wales using a comprehensive approach and the involvement of the local community.

Communities Plan: the Communities Plan (Sustainable Communities: Building for the Future) was launched on 5 February 2003. Sets out a long-term programme of action for delivering sustainable communities in both urban and rural areas, to tackle housing supply in the South East, low demand in other parts of the country, and the quality of public spaces.

Community Action: comprehensively, action by local people or communities of interest that aims to bring about change in people's lives, however large or small. In contrast to other approaches to community work, it can involve protest, confrontation, and sometimes direct action (see Chapter 2).

Community Action Network (CAN) develops, promotes and supports social entrepreneurs and their enterprises through the CAN Online server.

Community businesses: organizations that are established to provide services and/or employment in a local community, normally non-profit-making, as independent and self-supporting organizations.

Community Chest: Neighbourhood Renewal Community funds, administered by voluntary sector 'lead organizations', which give grants of up to £5,000 for projects to help work in their own neighbourhoods. It has now become part of the Single Regeneration Budget Programme.

Community cohesion: is a term that has become increasingly popular in public policy debates; closely linked to concepts such as inclusion and exclusion, social capital and differentiation, community and neighbourhood. A simple measure of community cohesion would be whether groups who live in a local area are actively getting together to promote or defend some common interest.

Community sector: the whole range of autonomous collective activity undertaken in neighbourhoods or by communities of interest, to improve collective life and conditions.

Experience-based learning: knowledge, skills and understanding acquired from doing something or having been involved in an activity or process.

Holistic approach to assessment: treating a learner's work as more than the sum of parts submitted and searching for and taking into account evidence presented throughout the process and assessing the overall impression.

Human resources: the people who can be drawn upon to contribute to a particular task.

Impairment: is a characteristic feature or attribute which restricts an individual's participation in society, and may be of the senses, mind or body. Disability arises from being prevented from participating socially through inadequate recognition and/or facilities for people's needs. Thus dealing with disability is as much a matter of social attitudes as of adequate provision.

Line management: overseeing the work done by those to whom it is delegated and ensuring that targets are met and that work being produced is of an adequate quality. A line manager may also provide supervision; but this may be provided by a non-managerial supervisor.

Local Strategic Partnerships: a Local Strategic Partnership (LSP) is a single non-statutory, multi-agency body, which matches local authority boundaries, and aims to bring together at local level the different parts of the public, private, community and voluntary sectors. Local partners working through an LSP will be expected to take many of the major decisions about priorities for their local area. <www.neighbourhood.gov.uk>.

National occupational standards: the levels of performance which people working in a particular field are expected to demonstrate. These are set by the relevant, often statutory, body and are obligatory for recognition in most pastoral, caring and community professions.

NVQs – National Vocational Qualifications: a practice-based route to qualification (SVQ in Scotland) usually offered by further education colleges through work-based learning.

Outcomes or outputs: the impact a group or project wants to have. They are usually set out in measurable terms so that they can be evaluated. They may be immediate, medium term or long term.

Processes of social change: involve working with communities to enable people to contribute their energies, initiatives and participation to the achievement of goals and to the definition of these goals; on a wider level, as professional groups and agencies incorporate community work ideas and skills into their work, to develop ways of working in partnership and developing approaches that facilitate the involvement of local people in decision-making.

Reflective practitioner: working in a manner that follows the action-reflection model of learning which involves thinking about work that has been done, applying lessons learnt both from mistakes and good practice and reflecting on the nature and purpose of the task(s) so as to inform and enhance future practice.

Regeneration: area-based development usually taking place on a time-limited basis.

Social capital: some quotes:

> Whereas physical capital refers to physical objects and human capital refers to the properties of individuals, social capital refers to connections among individuals and social networks and the norms of reciprocity and trustworthiness that arise from them. In that sense social capital is closely related to what some have called "civic virtue." The difference is that "social capital" calls attention to the fact that civic virtue is most powerful when embedded in a sense network of reciprocal social relations. A society of many virtuous but isolated individuals is not necessarily rich in social capital.
>
> (Putnam, Robert D., 2000. *Bowling Alone: the collapse and revival of American communities.* New York: Simon and Schuster)

> Social capital is not just the sum of the institutions which underpin a society – it is the glue that holds them together.
>
> (The World Bank. <www.infed.org>)

Social exclusion: the government has defined social exclusion as a shorthand label for what can happen when individuals or areas suffer from a combination of linked problems such as unemployment, poor health, low incomes, poor housing, high crime environments, bad health and family breakdown. It can also have a wider meaning which encompasses the exclusion of people from the normal exchanges, practices and rights of society. <www.socialexclusion>

Social inclusion: active involvement of disadvantaged and oppressed individuals, groups and communities so that they both feel and have the benefits of being part of the whole community.

Statutory sector: bodies that exist as a result of a Government statute or which carry out statutory requirements, such as local authorities and health authorities.

Strategic relationships: developing contacts or working with other individuals, groups or networks or agencies where there are specific benefits to the relationship (e.g. political, social, financial).

Strategic working: working collectively to a commonly agreed plan towards commonly agreed goals within a perspective that is wider than the individual or group itself.

Super Output Areas (SOAs): Super Output Areas (SOAs) are a new geographic hierarchy designed to improve the reporting of small area statistics in England and Wales.

Supervision: provision of support, reassurance and feedback in a framework that allows time to think about the work being done, the freedom to make mistakes and to have open discussions and ensure accountability to the organization. (See Chapters 7 and 9.)

Sure Start: a government scheme which aims to improve the well-being of families and children before and from birth, enabling them to benefit better when they go to school, by setting up programmes to improve services for families with children, spreading good practice learned from local programmes and providing services for young children. It is currently being reorganized. **Flying Start** is a similar programme for mothers and babies. <www.surestart.gov.uk>

Synergy: added value arising from the working together of various organizations.

Subject index

Index of scriptural references